Curriculum Lab
College of Education Health & Human Services
University of Michigan-Dearborn

S0-BBU-286

CREATIVE ART
for the
DEVELOPING
CHILD

CREATIVE ART
for the
DEVELOPING CHILD

A TEACHER'S HANDBOOK FOR EARLY
CHILDHOOD EDUCATION

SECOND EDITION

Clare Cherry

Curriculum Lab
College of Education Health & Human Services
University of Michigan-Dearborn

Photography by Samuel A. Cherry

Fearon Teacher Aids,
Simon & Schuster Supplementary Education Group

FOR LYNNE-TANYA AND NEELI

Photo on page 293 by Pat Roper

Copyright © 1972, 1990 by Fearon Teacher Aids. All rights reserved. Published 1972. Second Edition 1990. No part of this book may be reproduced by any means, transmitted, or translated into a machine language without written permission from the publisher.

ISBN 0-8224-1633-6

Library of Congress Catalog Card Number 89-85779

Printed in the United States of America
1. 9 8 7 6 5 4 3 2 1

cke
373.5044
c-1
9|15

Contents

Preface

Creative Art for the Developing Child was revised in order to add new activities and refine the original material, not to change it. This edition, like the first one, approaches art as a developmental process and presents activities that are appropriate for the average 4-year-old child to do without adult help. These activities are based on specific materials presented in a manner that allows children to use the materials in their own unique ways. These ways differ from individual to individual, according to age, development, motor skills, interest in the activity, past experiences, reaction to the environment, and motivation. Thus, even 2-year-olds can use the materials, but they do so in a much simpler manner than 4-year-olds. And there is, in fact, no upper age limit for the activities because older children and adults will bring their own unique experiences and interests to the projects.

If you are doing art activities that the children really like but that require much teacher assistance or that depend on patterns, models, and step-by-step "do it exactly like I do it" directions, you can use the approaches in this book to redesign the activities. Trust children to express their own creative ideas when given the encouragement and motivation to do so.

Allow children to use their own perceptions in developing their imagination and intuitive skills. Let them know that it is all right to express how they feel and to explore new ways to use materials. As they begin to understand that their individuality is appreciated, and as you begin to understand that their standards are not the same as your standards, the right and left hemispheres of the brain will become integrated and creativity will flourish.

Thanks to the staff and children of Congregation Emanu El Clare Cherry School in San Bernardino, California, for their assistance in this revision. Thanks to Barbara Harkness for her contribution on repetition (pp. 12–13). And as always, thanks to my partner and husband, Sam, for the eloquent photographs and the new cover— with an apology to my grandson, Dani, now a professional artist, for relegating his famous cover photo to an interior page.

Preface to the First Edition

This book deals directly with ways in which creative art becomes developmental art and, as such, part of the entire growth process of the child—and of the creative growth of you, the teacher, as well. The program described in this book is based on trust, honesty, and acceptance. It is self-starting, self-pacing, and goal directed toward academic and personal achievement. My approach is a personal one, based on more than 25 years of experience with children's art.

The children I refer to in this book are between 2 and 6 years of age. As children grow, they become able to make certain physical movements at sequential stages of their development. These movements relate to their sensory awareness and their capacity to perceive, which are avenues to cognition. There is, then, to a certain degree, a predictable sequence in the development of perception and cognition in children, although the precise age at which any specific development takes place varies from child to child. The activities in this book take account of this developmental sequence.

With few exceptions, every activity in this book can be pursued by 4-year-olds without adult assistance. Many of the activities suggested on these pages are somewhat complex for 2-year-olds and should be simplified when used with this age group. Many 3-year-olds, however, can do the same work as 4-year-olds, and some 5-year-olds have advanced no further in some areas than the level achieved by some 4-year-olds. Occasional reference is made to older children, meaning children who are in kindergarten or the first grade. Actually, there is no upper age limit for the use of the material presented in this book. Because the program relies primarily on the choice of materials and the way in which they are presented, children of *any* age may pursue the activities in accordance with their own abilities and at their own levels of creative growth.

The key to meeting children's needs is your ability to question, listen, and respond—to respond to their answers, movements, feelings, and moods. Being responsive requires being sensitive to their behavior—to restlessness or exuberance, to loneliness or withdrawal, to hurt, joy, impatience, and wonder. Being responsive requires being sensitive to all the feelings and needs the children bring to school with them—and recognizing your own feelings and needs as well. The aim of this book is to encourage teachers—and parents—to be responsive—to use this key not only to meet the needs of developing children but also to help unlock their creative potential.

Throughout the book I have listed the probable growth that will occur as a result of the child's participation in each particular activity. These lists should by no means be considered as separate entities. Each activity is interrelated with many other activities. Learning that takes place in the creative art program is the cumulative result of many experiences and many repetitions of these experiences.

This book could not have become a reality without the contributions, both knowing and unknowing, of so many persons. My greatest debt is to the children I have had the joy of working with throughout the years. They have taught me whatever I know today about creative art for the developing child. Also, it is a privilege to have this opportunity to express my deepest appreciation and thanks to Congregation Emanu El for allowing me the freedom for research and for the support given to the exploratory program that has been developed in the school sponsored by the Congregation. I am grateful to the classroom teachers with whom I have worked—Aileen Applebaum, Lael Cohen, Barbie Gaines, Bettye Kovitz, Mary McDermott, Janet Peters, Alyce Smothers, Barbara Stangle, Halliette Stubbs, and Helen Wallick—all of whom tried out, added to, and encouraged my constant search for methods of presenting and evaluating developmental art. I also wish to thank Dr. Martha Frank for first alerting me to the young child as a medium for creative pursuit; Dr. Donald Churchill, Betty Fauth, Barbara Harkness, Dr. Nikolai Khokhlov, and Betty Zelman for their professional advice; Don Emkens for his darkroom work; Rabbis Norman F. Feldheym and Hillel Cohn for their wise counsel; and the many participating parents who lent their varied talents in so many ways. I also want to thank my husband, not only for his fine photographs, which illustrate this book, but for the frequent exchanges of ideas that made each difficult task seem suddenly easier.

CHAPTER 1

The Developmental Art Program

Bobby was in his first week of nursery school. Each day when he came home, his mother asked, "What did you do today?" His usual answer was, "Oh, nothing. I just played." Then one day he brought home a painting he had made.

He had enjoyed dipping the long-handled brush into the can of creamy red paint. He had enjoyed smearing it back and forth and back and forth over the sheet of paper his teacher had given him. He discovered that if he pressed very hard and rubbed the brush in one little area, he could rub a hole right through the paper. He didn't understand why the teacher gave him the paper to take home. He had already made the hole. Besides, the paint was dry. Dry paint wasn't fun.

But Bobby's mother was excited when she saw it. So was his father. And even the lady who lived next door. But, oh, especially his mother. She told the teacher glowingly how much everyone liked Bobby's picture. Sensing that she had pleased Bobby's mother, the teacher had the child paint another picture the very next day. She soon began to give him more and more art projects to do, and they became more and more complicated. Sometimes the teacher had to do much of the work herself, with only a little help from Bobby. Bobby's mother told everyone about the wonderful teacher Bobby had and about the wonderful school he attended and about the wonderful things he made there.

The teacher was very capable and understanding, but she literally got carried away with her attempt to please Bobby's mother. Bobby's mother was also a very capable and under-standing person—but Bobby was always restless and he had been slow in his early growth. His mother had worried about his ability to do well in school. She was delighted and im-pressed when she saw the wonderful art projects he was bringing home, even though she really knew he couldn't do them by himself.

And so, somewhere between the interweaving of adult dreams and adult anxieties, a little boy's needs were being forgotten.

And what about the little boy? Was he learning anything through doing one complicated art project after another? Well, he was learning how to please adults. He learned that blue at the top of the picture means sky. Circles have to contain eyes, noses, and mouths. When the teacher cuts out something for you to paste, you do it exactly the way she shows you to—after all, she knows what she wants you to make. He learned not to let the paint drip. And he learned that above all—oh, above all—he mustn't ever rub a real hole in the paper.

Each time the children enter the classroom, they will find many activity areas where they can go and start exploring. These areas will be different from day to day and week to week according to the weather, the season, the number of students, the development of the curriculum, the acquisition of new equipment and supplies, the mood of the children, and the teacher's mood as well. The children will find blocks. Puzzles and manipulative games. Science materials. Things to take apart, connect, stack, fit, sort, arrange, count, divide, balance. Dolls to bathe. Hats to wear. Places to be with others. Places to be alone. Musical instruments. Suitcases to pack and carry. Special things for special days. And *each* day is a special day.

Not only will the materials and equipment be changed from time to time, but the places where the children find certain things will also be changed occasionally. This kind of variety challenges them to develop new ideas and ways of doing things. But enough things will always remain the same to ensure their security and the comfort of knowing, understanding, and belonging.

Small groups form. If children find there is no room for them at one particular activity center, they will eagerly approach another area, because the room is full of challenging things, rich with potentialities for many kinds of learnings.

Conversations spring up among the children and between the children and the adults. Sometimes, however, one child or two or an entire group may become so deeply engrossed in creative thought that there is very little talking.

Here and there among the activity centers the children will find art materials. A table with collage materials is on one side of the room. Crayons and paper are on another table. Out of the mainstream of traffic, but obvious, open, and inviting, are areas for painting and for clay manipulation.

The teacher is busy moving throughout the room. She helps one child along a walking board. Another needs his shoes tied. She shares the laughter of two children as they watch a too-high tower of interlocking cubes come tumbling down. Perhaps she discusses with them why it tumbled. She stops to put names on the papers of the children working at the collage table. She helps a child using crayons to spell her own name. And she keeps a watchful eye on the painters and the clay manipulators, assisting them if they need assistance, commenting on the way they are handling the materials, helping them to be fair in taking turns, and generally sharing their feelings as they work. Comments such as "That bright yellow looks even brighter next to the purple, doesn't it?" or "I see you made a wavy design" are appropriate. Her comments about the actual art work are factual, not evaluative. It is perfectly acceptable, however, to express a positive evaluation of the children's *behavior*. The teacher might say, "I like the way you always put the brush back in the same can it came from," or "I like the way you are sharing the clay," or even, "I'm glad you've learned to share the clay." There are two important reasons to talk to the children as they work. First, factual comments about their work help children to form concepts and to relate what they are doing to other areas of the curriculum. Second, evaluative comments about their behavior help children to grow in self-awareness. When such comments are positive, they elevate the children's self-esteem.

A sense of happy and meaningful play, movement, and accomplishment pervades the atmosphere. The teacher had come early enough to arrange the room and prepare the needed materials before the class session began. Therefore, she is able to fully enjoy, with the children, the free flow of activity from one area to another. The session is a beautiful and touching ballet of forms, colors, people, and rhythm.

Art education is a meaningful force in this total learning program. By sensitive planning, the children are motivated to pursue art activities and enjoy experiences that lead to general overall development. Having plenty of time to move from one step of growth to another at their own pace and in accordance with their own abilities and interests helps the children develop strong feelings of self-esteem and self-confidence. As they grow to recognize their own individuality, they become better equipped to withstand the emotional pressures of overly structured situations that they will encounter throughout life. Having many opportunities to become deeply involved in experiences related to touch, smell, vision, and hearing facilitates the children's sensorimotor development. Continuous opportunities lead to perceptual growth and subsequently to greater cognition. As you acquire an understanding of the developmental process of growth of young children, you will more fully appreciate your own role in the classroom and your ability to guide children through wholesome experiences.

THE DEVELOPMENTAL GROWTH OF THE YOUNG CHILD

Research indicates that there is a predictable *sequence* in the development of children's art. Many factors enter into these predictions, and many contradictory opinions have developed. Relating this sequence to the way children develop physically, however, makes the development of children's art easy to understand, because children can use their arms and hands to draw or paint only in accordance with the development of their neuromotor systems.

At birth, infants have no control over specific movements. Rather, they depend on reflexes. Very soon the process of learning to control movement begins, however, starting at the base of the neck and gradually moving outward (cephalocaudal development) and downward (proximodistal development). Thus, the first sign of control of movement is that of holding the head upright. Gradually the control moves to the shoulders. By 3 months of age, most infants can throw their shoulders in one direction strongly enough to turn themselves over. Meanwhile, the ability to control movement has also moved downward, so that by that age an infant is able to use the shoulders and upper chest to begin the process of lifting the upper body upward when lying on the stomach. The control of arm movements moves from the shoulders down the upper arm during the first year of life. If you stand a year-old infant in front of a wall with a paintbrush in his hand, the infant will wield the brush up and down or from side to side in a pumplike motion. Parts of the arm are not yet differentiated. By 1½ years of age, children usually have gained control as far down as their elbows. Thus, we find children of this age making lovely sweeping arcs with paint or crayon—since that is the shape that comes out when elbow movements are practiced. It isn't until age 2½ that the control of movement reaches the wrist. At that age, children universally start making circular motions in their scribbles, the result of having practiced wrist movements.

Crayon scribbles by children between 2 years 4 months of age and 5 years 1 month.
Children's ability to scribble develops in direct relation to their ability to control their
movements and to their awareness of the relationship between themselves and the
space around them. Their marks become progressively more complex as their muscle
control develops. The sequence of psychomotor development is approximately the
same for each child.

7

CIRCLES

Gradually, as development continues, children become able to control their movements more and more. The lines they draw show curves and ovals and spirals, and the lines may begin to run in horizontal or diagonal directions. Although children's earliest scribbles are mere accidents of movement while holding pencils or crayons, they soon begin to recognize that it is *their* movements that cause the marks to appear on the paper. At this time they experience the thrill of making something that was not there before. The pleasure derived from this discovery encourages children to work to develop even greater skills. They learn that they can make daubs and scratches and marks, which they often repeat over and over in one area until they have internalized a particular movement pattern.

As they continue to practice, young scribblers next become aware of the circles they are able to make. They learn to perceive the circles as distinct shapes. From birth, the human eye responds favorably to circular or oval shapes similar to the shape of the human head and the nipples on a mother's breasts. The circle is a gentle shape, natural and elemental. From ancient times, it has been used as a symbol of the Self, the psyche. Children's egos and their awareness of themselves as individuals begin to surface just about the same time they are developing the ability to draw circular patterns. As the children's awareness of their ability to control their movements grows, they begin trying things out, inventing things to do, and experimenting with this ability.

MANDALAS AND SUNS

When children begin to be able to direct some of the smaller muscles of the hand, their drawings become more complex. Circles become mandalas or radials. Many of the drawings resemble suns. The drawings become more complex as children increase their ability to move their fingers in more complicated motions. They like the circles they can make, so they decorate them with lines and crosses or other marks. Children's ability to control their movements and to relate to the world increases. Then, one day they draw a person.

SYMBOLS

The notion that children's first figures are merely oversized heads with legs and arms added is one of the most common misconceptions about children's art. Think of the last time you saw a child draw such figures. Did the child know that hands do not grow out of the ears? Of course. The circles were never meant to be heads in the first place. As far as children are concerned, the circle is the person, the symbol, the complete figure. They may place facial features as a means of identifying the symbol, but it is frequently an adult who first says, "Where are the hands?" Since children don't find it necessary to separate the body from the head, they will usually place the hands near the top of the symbol where the shoulders would be if the head and body had been drawn separately. If you ask about legs, the child may accommodate you by drawing a pair, even if the symbol was not meant to be a person at all. Perhaps it is a car, or a tree, or even a house. But in the developing imagination of a young child, a car, a tree, or even a house can have legs.

VISUAL-MOTOR DEVELOPMENT

As growth continues, development moves from the wrist to the fingertips when children are 5 or 5½ years of age. Only then

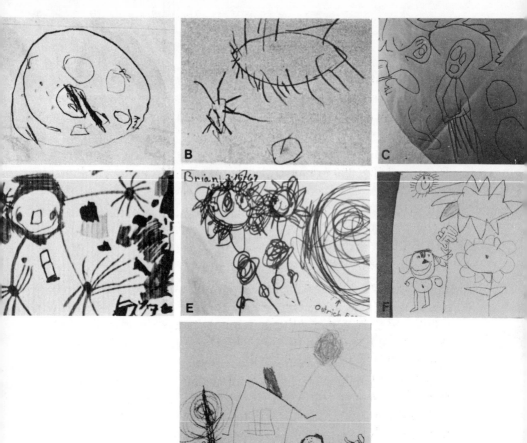

Symbolic drawings by children between 3 years of age and 5 ½. While children are progressing
through the scribbling sequence, they are also beginning to experiment with symbolization,
which eventually leads to pure representation. *Picture A* is a series of circles drawn by a 3-year-
old, who apparently recognizes his ability to use them as symbols. As children develop, they
decorate their circles with rays and appendages of all kinds, as we see in *B* and *C,* which turn
them into suns, flowers, and people. In *Picture D,* Laura's figure has hands and fingers, legs and
toes. She has made the arms different lengths in order to accommodate them to the available
space, which is disproportionate as a result of her starting her drawing so far to the left. To
balance the figure, she has filled the remaining space with a colorful design. In *Picture E,* Brian
identified his circle as an ostrich egg (the teacher wrote the words for him). The two figures with
elongated necks may therefore be ostriches. (When children first discover how to draw necks,
they become very conscious of them and exaggerate them in their drawings.) In *Picture F,* the
child has used the circle in all the universal patterns, combining sun, cloud, tree, flower, and
person in one design. *Picture G,* by a 5½-year-old, shows the child's growing need to
communicate. This picture of his environment—including the artist riding a tricycle—tells as
complete a story as any written composition.

10

can they have full control over the entire hand and perform the complex movements that misguided adults often asked them to perform at an earlier age. Simultaneously with the development of arm and hand movements, children are learning to control the movements of other parts of the body as well, including the eyes. The normal human eye takes in almost everything that comes into the range of its visual field, but we can *understand* what we see only after we have learned to integrate the sensory input.

As children grow, they learn that things can move toward them and away from them. They begin to develop a sequence of skills, each dependent upon those that came before. They learn the concepts of up and down in relation to their own bodies and then in relation to other objects. Later, children learn the concepts of left and right, not by those words at first, but at least in relation to their own bodies.

One of the steps in normal child development is the acquisition of *laterality*—knowing that one has two sides to the body, but that one side is the dominant, or controlling side. In order to achieve laterality, children have to learn that they have a middle—which requires learning that they have a left side and a right side (although they don't have to be able to name those sides), a top and a bottom, and a front and a back. The middle, the imaginary line where the right and left halves meet, is called the *midline.* Unless appropriate development has occurred, a child may avoid crossing the midline and will twist the torso or change the hand in use in order to avoid doing so. When appropriate development has occurred, both the right and the left hemisphere of the brain are equally involved. (For more information about appropriate development and the brain, see Cherry, Godwin, and Staples, *Is the Left Brain Always Right?* Fearon Teacher Aids, 1989.)

While they are acquiring these skills, children learn to coordinate eye movement to produce an integrated image. This coordination is perfected through basic movement patterns; for this reason, eye-hand activities, such as those required in most art projects, are very important to children's overall growth.

Eye-hand activities, together with the other natural movements of the body as experienced through play, gradually lead children to understand additional concepts, such as big and little, wide and narrow, over and under, smallest and tallest, behind and in front of, next to and farther away. As children learn to combine the control of their movements with these maturing perceptions, their scribbles, paintings, designs, and arrangements begin to take on pictorial rather than symbolic aspects. Their understanding of shapes is now combined with a deeper understanding of three-dimensional forms. As they approach this level of development, children are still perceiving things from a viewpoint that is different from that of an adult, however. Because we know the developmental sequence of children's sensorimotor growth and thinking, we can appreciate this difference. Although we motivate, support, and reinforce children's activities, we allow them the satisfaction of making discoveries without adult interference.

THE VALUE OF REPETITION

A common misconception in the classroom is that the children need to have a new type of art project or different art materials each day. In desperation, teachers resort to patterns and other people's cutouts, as well as to many inappropriate craft projects, in the quest for something "new."

In actuality, young children like repetition. They love hearing the same stories over and over again. You can play the same favorite records day after day or sing the same favorite songs, and the children won't tire of them. If you watch your students on the playground or listen to them play at housekeeping, you will find that children love repeating the same games and scenarios over and over.

When a new media is introduced or a new way of using a familiar media is presented, allow children to become totally immersed in it. Repeat the same experience every day for a week or two—or even for an entire month. Or repeat the experience once or twice a week over a period of months. Or repeat the activity several times in one day and then do it again as a follow up one or two times on another day. Make up your own combinations, based on the interest and mood of the children. Vary the activity slightly as you repeat it, in order to motivate thought. Listen to the children and make additions or modifications according to their ideas—or allow the children to make their own additions and modifications.

If you use the shape and color guides (pp. 42–46 and 58–61), don't hesitate in March or April to reintroduce a shape or color combination from October or November. Or, for example, if you use pennant shapes as suggested for November, you can keep a few pennant-shaped pieces of paper nearby your new art activities throughout the year so that children may use them if they wish to. Always keep in mind that when children are given the time and opportunity to repeat activities and internalize experiences, they are also intensifying the learning that is occurring.

EVALUATING THE CHILD'S PROGRESS

To enlarge the scope of your art program, evaluate your materials, the room environment, and your techniques. As your program develops, look for and encourage the children's increasing awareness of their growing creativity and skills. By dating the children's work, you can save representative examples over a period of time to assist you in recognizing and evaluating each child's progress. Evaluate this progress, however, only in accordance with the way the materials were presented to the children and *how* they reacted.

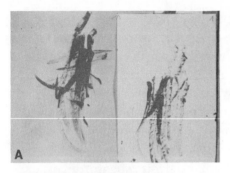

A

B

E

Paintings by children between 1½ years of age and 5 ½. In Painting A, we see two different paintings made on two different days by a 1½-year-old. His marks are the result of moving the whole arm in a pumplike motion, which is typical of that age. *Painting B* was done by the same child 4 months later. He has learned to use his elbow while painting and takes great delight in the arc-like marks that are the result of moving his arm horizontally. In *Painting C,* we can see that the marks made by a 2½-year-old are beginning to expand into ovals, and in *Painting D,* they take full circular form. In *Painting E,* circular masses have given way to linear experiments, and mandalas have begun to take shape. *Painting F* shows the next stage of development, the growing

G

I

J

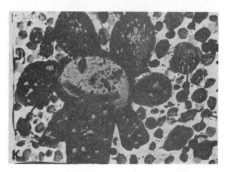

urge to cover the entire sheet of paper. Children spend many weeks exploring ways of doing this. Eventually, out of the solid mass of paint, new forms begin to take shape. In *Painting G,* mandalas and other types of circular shapes reappear as the child explores new linear strokes. In *Painting H,* we can see that the child has done considerable planning to produce an intricate design. This careful planning shows even further development in *Painting I,* which is a harmonious blending of various shades of brown, yellow, and orange. *Painting J* reveals even greater development on the part of a child somewhat older than any of the previous artists. When the legs of the figure turned out to be too short to reach the ground, the artist did not lengthen them out of proportion to make them reach. Rather, she filled the space around the legs with an intricate design, which brought the entire figure down to ground level. In *Painting K,* the design painted by a 5½-year-old in eight different colors is a joyful expression of self-esteem.

Avoid the pitfall of trying to read deep psychological meanings into children's paintings and drawings. Consider instead *all* of the circumstances under which a particular picture was made, and take care not to impose your own prejudices on your interpretation. For example, certain colors have traditional meanings in our society. We know that children have a tremendous reaction to color and that their paintings are influenced by the colors they choose. However, young children are not yet integrated into our culture to the extent that they are motivated by tradition when they choose a given color. Though children may be somewhat guided by emotion, they are limited to choosing from the colors that have been put out for them to use. Even so, a common misconception is that children who frequently use black are depressed or troubled. These children may indeed be depressed or troubled, but their problems may show more in the way they move—in their postures or facial expressions or in the way they apply the paint or divide the paper—than in their choice of color. The fact is that 2½-year-olds will explain using black by saying that "it looks good." What they may mean is that black shows up better than other colors and they like their pictures to be noticed.

Watch when 3- or 4-year-olds choose black in place of other colors. It may be the color that is closest to the easel. Or they may choose black because the teacher—perhaps because of her own fears—seldom offers it, which makes the color new and exciting to them. Once they select black, the children may get carried away with the dramatic impact it makes in relation to the other colors they have already used. After covering most of a picture with black, a 3- or 4-year-old might tell you "It's night" or "It's a big black dog." Or even "It's a man watering the lawn and his breakfast is ready." We must remember that children's perceptions are not the same as those of adults. In all probability, children cover pictures with black paint because black paint, especially tempera, is so emphatic and opaque and positive. Using it makes them feel quite important.

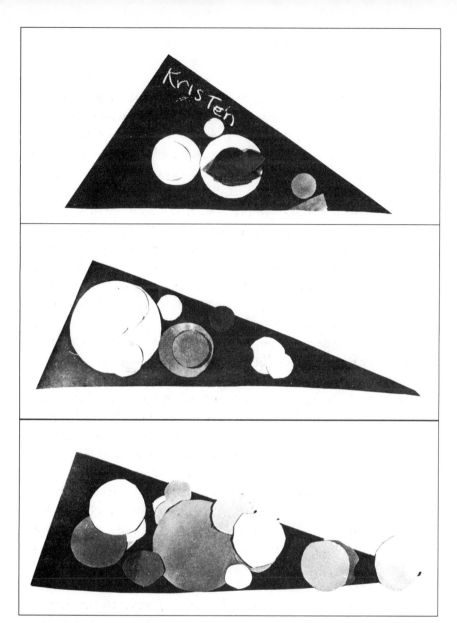

Collage development. The bottom sample was made by a 3½-year-old on her first day at school. She pasted the circles on at random and was not influenced by the shape of the cardboard. The middle piece, made by the same child two days later, shows that she has begun to grasp the concept of seriation in that she started her work with large circles at the large end of the pennant and proceeded to use smaller circles as she moved toward the small end. She also stacked smaller circles on top of larger ones, which she did not do in her first one. In the top sample, Kristen (4) solved the problem of where to place a paper ring that would not fit on the pennant without overlapping by folding it to fit over a circle that she had already pasted on.

What you should evaluate in children's work is the progress they make from one month to the next in their

- division and arrangement of space,
- awareness of shapes,
- ability to control hand and finger movements in coordination with eye movements, and
- sensitivity to the materials.

In looking for these signs of progress, you will become aware of an emerging sense of color, balance, design, and, above all, creative imagination and inventiveness. You will learn to accept the reality that the creative process is an individual process, that art is a medium that stimulates growth, and that each child must be allowed the privilege of learning through personal experiences.

IMPLEMENTING THE CREATIVE ART PROGRAM

The type of material that children use in the creative art program is not the most important consideration. What they create with these materials is not the most important aspect either. *The opportunity to use the materials freely is what counts in creative developmental art. In order to build creativity, the process must always take precedence over the finished product.*

Freedom, however, does not mean that the children are to function without direction. As in all areas of life, things run more smoothly when everyone involved knows what is expected of them. In the creative art program, both adults and children will benefit from the existence of ground rules. A few important guidelines for the teacher are offered in the following paragraphs.

Keeping Hands Off. Once you have prepared and presented the materials, allow the children to do all the work themselves. Let them do it the way they want to do it. Encourage them to explore, experiment, change, and originate. If you have given the children some guidelines for a particular kind of project, let them decide whether to follow your suggestions or to branch off in an original direction.

Being Involved. Even though you allow the children to work on a project and use materials in their own way, you should still show that you are interested in what they do. Make them feel comfortable in what they are doing by your sincere show of friendship. The children know that your presence will help them keep their behavior within acceptable limits. Your interest in and appreciation of their projects will inspire them when they need additional motivation or reassurance.

Helping Children Please Themselves. Help the children understand that they need only to please themselves with what they create. Help them to know that they are the sole owners of their creations. If you want to keep your students' work and display it, ask their permission.

Offering Help. Offer to help the children learn skills if they indicate a desire and need for such help. Offer help if they lose control of the materials they are using. Also offer to help them care for their finished products at the conclusion of the activity.

Interpreting to Parents. Help parents to understand the purpose of creative developmental art. Explain the developmental and educational goals. Explain the ground rules. Show the parents by your attitude that you sincerely appreciate each child's efforts. Prepare art displays. Help the parents to understand that the purpose of the children's art work is not just to make something to take home, but rather to meet the developmental goals of childhood and to expand the educational program.

At the beginning of each school year, it is a good idea to notify the parents about the essentials of your art program so that they will understand the goals of developmental activities you will be providing. You might send them a letter like the following one.

Dear Parents,

Your child will be participating in a developmental art program geared toward accumulating skills that will be important to future academic accomplishments. The goal of our art program is to motivate and challenge children to use an ever-changing variety of art media in ways that will enhance specific areas of development. Attached is a list of many of the types of learning that occur when children are allowed to be their own inventors.

We seldom provide patterns. What your child brings home will be his or her response to the materials provided. What your child creates will be based on his or her interests, needs, skills, developmental age, imagination, and sometimes even what other children are observed doing with the materials.

We suggest that when children bring their art work home, you comment about the colors, the mood, the lines, or the art media itself. If you always say only "That's a pretty picture," that response will soon become meaningless to the child. "Do you want to tell me about that interesting picture?" is a better question than "What is it?" Asking what a picture is may imply to the child that art always has to represent a particular thing. Art, however, can also be a design, an expression of a mood, or an exploration of media. Specific comments about your child's work can be very meaningful, for example:

"I can see that you worked hard to cover the whole paper."
"I like the way you left some of the white paper showing."
"That yellow and red look good next to each other."
"I like those wavy purple lines. They make me feel happy."
"Those dots make it look like your brush was dancing on the paper."
"The colors of the crayons you used look good in our kitchen."
"Those shapes must have been hard to make."

Making specific observations about your child's work not only shows an interest but also acknowledges the artistic process.

Occasionally, we will clip a note to your child's art work to tell you about a specific detail of it. Please respond accordingly.

Thank you,
The Staff

Examples of Types of Learning That Occur in a Developmental Art Program

- Eye-hand coordination and fine motor skills
- Visual-motor skills
- Control of muscular tension
- Participation in group projects
- Discrimination among different shapes; among different colors, shades, and intensities of color; among various sizes and spaces; among various quantities and weights
- Sequencing
- Arranging
- Planning in advance
- Responsibility for materials and surroundings
- Problem solving
- Decision making
- Inventing
- Imagining
- Awareness of linear patterns, color contrasts, spatial relationships, cause and effect, time, quantity and proportion, texture, measurements, reversibility of a process, gravity

In a developmental art program, children develop the self-esteem that comes with accomplishment, the imagination that comes with experimentation, and the motor control that comes with practice.

A Note About Art for the Holidays

In preschools, holidays should be observed as simply as possible. Young children are often overexposed to holiday observances. The excitement can lead to emotional overstimulation and sometimes to physical exhaustion.

Most teachers, including me, have used traditional holiday motifs and symbols over and over again. There is a need in our lives for tradition and comfort in the use of familiar symbols. Too great an emphasis on traditional form, however, may discourage creativity. It is possible to enrich the children's lives by encouraging creative experiences in holiday art.

Any of the ideas that are discussed in this book may be used in holiday art projects. Through the use of appropriate colors, special papers, and other materials, your everyday art projects can take on a seasonal air. They will reflect the spirit of the traditional motifs, whether or not recognizable symbols are used. You will find suggestions in the sections "Paper Shapes Through the Year" in Chapter 2 and "Color Guide Through the Year" in Chapter 3.

GROUND RULES FOR THE CHILDREN

The ground rules for the children are more specific than those for the adult. Their purpose is to ensure the safety of the children and the functioning of the class.

1. The children must understand that tools must be handled with care. They will usually do so if you show them by your attitude that you sincerely trust them to do so.
2. The children must know that they may not use the art materials for touching or hitting other children or adults.
3. The children must be aware that art materials are not to be wasted, and that they are for use only in creating art work.
4. Art materials must not be thrown, deliberately spilled, or destroyed.
5. The children are not to put paste, paint, glue, chalk, or any other art material in their mouth. The materials are not for tasting, eating, or drinking.
6. The children must also know that art materials are to be kept in the art area.
7. Everyone works on his or her own project and does not interfere with the work of other children.
8. Painting and other art work is done only on the materials provided for that purpose.
9. Clothing and other children are not to be deliberately painted on.

Within these limits, everyone involved has greater freedom for self-direction and for self-pacing than if there were no guidelines at all or if the limits were too many and too restricting.

YOUR ROLE IN THE CLASSROOM

By carefully setting ground rules, you can be free to help the children make the fullest use, according to their needs, of the art materials offered to them. You can help them to be sensitive and understanding by being sensitive and understanding yourself. You can help the children develop habits of observation, questioning, and listening by your own examples of observation, questioning, and listening. Help them to become aware of their feelings and to know that it is all right to express them and that sometimes feelings can be channeled into nonverbal means of expression. Help the children to know that they are free to make choices and that, as long as they demonstrate consideration for people and things, they do not always have to conform. Help them to know that their independent thoughts and spontaneous actions are appreciated and that imagination is a wonderful thing to have.

THE ROOM ENVIRONMENT

The ground rules will be easier to follow and the developmental goals will be easier to achieve if they are taken into account in planning the room environment. As much thought must be given to the appearance of the room as to its function and use. Even an old building can be enriched by painting the rooms in light, neutral tones. The addition of brightly colored accessories, which are more readily renewable than the basic equipment, will set off the neutral tones of the older pieces.

To help foster creativity and appreciation of color and design, make use of bulletin boards as an integral part of the creative teaching program (Cherry, *Nursery School Bulletin Boards,* Fearon Teacher Aids, 1973). Colors, arrangements, textures, and content should be changed frequently to reflect the time of the year, class activities, special events, and the progress of the class. Each new display, each picture change, however, should be handled just as carefully and arranged with as much thought as though the room were being prepared for the opening day of school. Many objects may be displayed around the room. These items should emphasize the effect of color, line, unusual beauty, or some other aesthetic value. Some simple rules should be kept in mind in planning the room environment and displaying the children's work.

1. Always remember that the child's eye level is much lower than that of the adult. Displays should therefore be placed low, where the children can approach, touch, feel, and even smell them at will.
2. A child-oriented room environment leaves plenty of undecorated wall space to allow the children freedom to use their own imaginations.
3. When children's work is displayed, it must not be "improved on" by the teacher for the purpose of impressing other adults. This applies not only to displaying finished work, but also to any work that is to be used as part of a larger display. Sometimes a teacher will, for example, cut a child's painting to form leaves, flowers, or other decorative designs. This should not be done unless the child did the work *expressly for this purpose.*
4. When displays are changed, the teacher should always leave some areas unchanged so that the children will not feel uncomfortable in what may appear to them to be new surroundings. The teacher should change enough things at one time, however, to stimulate and encourage imaginative thinking.
5. From time to time, display reproductions of famous paintings or original art by professional artists. No comments on them are needed except in response to the children's questions. After an artist's work has been displayed for two or three weeks, you might want to then give the class some simple biographical information about the artist.

DISPLAYING CHILDREN'S ART WORK

Displaying children's art work lets them know that you really like it and that you consider their creative efforts to be of value.

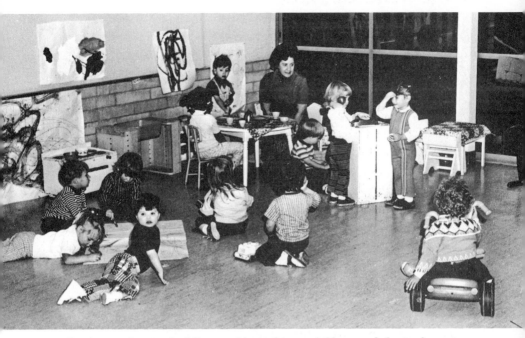

One corner of a room for 2 ¹/₂-year-olds. At this age children need plenty of room to move around in and many activity areas to explore. No area of the room should detract from any other area. The photograph on the first page of this chapter shows a room for 4- and 5-year-olds.

Matting or framing their art work will make the display more attractive. Don't allow the lack of time to prepare mats prevent you, however, from putting the children's work up where it can be seen. Simple mats can be easily made from paper.

How to Make a Simple Mat

To make a mat, use a piece of construction paper, fadeless art paper, or any other paper that is larger than the picture that is to be mounted. Select a color that harmonizes with one of the colors in the picture, or use black or white, both of which are always effective and will harmonize with almost any picture. Mount the picture on the mat by simply attaching it with pins, two-sided tape, transparent tape, or rubber cement. (Rubber cement will not cause the paper to shrink or wrinkle, but most other kinds of paste or glue will.)

The Display

Display the matted or framed pictures in groups mounted on corrugated display cardboard, posterboard, illustration board, or on the bulletin board. The pictures in each group should have similar mats or frames and should be arranged in a way that will provide an overall pattern of harmony.

Pictures can be grouped according to the ages of the children who made them, in order to show the developmental progress of child art, or they can be grouped according to kinds of projects, in order to show the variety of activities in which the children have participated. The best way to handle multicolored displays is to group the pictures according to their dominant color.

ARRANGEMENT OF FURNISHINGS

The room should be arranged in such a way that it can be kept neat and orderly even when many different activities are going on at the same time. By keeping arrangements flexible, by considering convenience as well as attractiveness, and by helping the children learn to assume responsibility for the appearance of the classroom, an orderly environment can be easily maintained. In a neat and orderly environment, children's minds are not cluttered and confused by disorder, and they are freer to release their own imaginative thoughts and to produce creative works.

CUPBOARDS AND STORAGE CONTAINERS

Cupboards and other storage areas should be given as much attention as the appearance of the rest of the room. Keeping storage areas neat and attractive need take only a few minutes each day.

Storage containers should be in harmony with the other

colors used in the room. One coat of vinyl paint or one strip of decorative Con-Tact paper can work wonders with a cardboard box. Other attractive storage units can be made from

- transparent plastic shoe storage boxes,
- refrigerator storage containers,
- colorful baskets, and
- painted cigar boxes.

If the storage units have some uniformity of size, it is easier to arrange them neatly. Label everything for ease in finding what you want when it is needed.

THE ART AREA

The art area may be a permanent place in the classroom, or its location may be changed from time to time. Since the types of activities will vary from day to day, the art area should be able to accommodate the materials and activities that will be involved. Certain requirements for the art area, however, always hold true. It should be

- away from the main flow of room traffic but not isolated from other activities in the room,
- well lit,
- close to a source of water, if water is needed,
- easy to supervise,
- large enough for each child to work in comfort,
- away from any unprotected surfaces that are hard to clean, and
- large enough to have a place for drying paintings and placing other finished work.

When repeating various art activities, change the way you set up the art area to renew the excitement of exploration and self-discovery. Sometimes you can limit the number of children who may work at a given area to one or two at a time. On other occasions you can set up the art area in such a way that several children can participate at the same time.

Even a slight change in table arrangements, materials, and supplies can add excitement and stimulation to the program. Never change things so drastically, however, that the children are faced with unfamiliarity; just make subtle changes in position, angle, background materials, container, location, or procedure.

CHILD PROOFING

The area used for creative experiences should be so arranged and planned that you will not have to spend your time admonishing everyone to "be careful" or "watch out."

- If the working surface is not washable and the medium being used is spillable, splashable, or stainable, the surface can be protected by a plastic covering.
- Use dropcloths, plastic sheets, newspapers, or other coverings to protect the floor during very messy activities.
- Paper or plastic sheets can also be taped to adjacent walls to protect them from being splattered.
- A pail of water and plenty of sponges and paper towels should be readily available for emergency cleanups.
- Keep a broom, a mop, a dustpan, and similar equipment nearby.

CHILD PROTECTION

Protect the children from having to worry about getting dirty. They will be more comfortable and work more freely if they

The art cart. It is mounted on casters so that it can be easily moved from room to room or into the storage closet. The supplies can be changed at any time.

know that their school clothes are adequately protected from art materials by aprons, smocks, or other coveralls. Such items may be commercially purchased, homemade out of plastic, or made from adult blouses or shirts, worn backward, with the sleeves cut off.

Long sleeves on children's clothing should be rolled up, and it may be necessary to take off sweaters during an art activity so that the children feel comfortable and free to move.

WATER

If the children cannot easily reach running water, keep one or two plastic buckets of warm water close by. Add a small quantity of mild soap as a disinfectant. Provide sponges and paper towels. If the children give their hands a preliminary rinsing in the classroom, they can wash them more thoroughly in the lavatory, without getting paint on the walls and doors on the way there.

MATERIALS

Although materials should not be wasted, you should set out enough so that the children will be able to complete their projects. Sufficient quantities of materials should be ready *before* the class begins. You should never have to interrupt an activity to prepare additional materials. Too many materials, however, can be confusing to children. Experiment to find the appropriate amount usually needed.

QUALITY

Materials should be of good quality. Even when budgets are severely limited, you should not skimp on the quality of paints, paper, and other materials. It is better to offer certain art experiences less often if budget considerations pose a problem than to have children produce wishy-washy work due to poor materials. For example, the children do not have to use paints every day. The painting experience will be far more valuable if the paints are in ample supply and sparkling with color, even if they can be used only once or twice a week. Ways to get the most out of paint materials and to expand the children's opportunities for creative self-expression with less expensive materials, such as newsprint and crayons, are presented in subsequent chapters.

As often as possible, set out only the raw ingredients for the art or craft projects and let the children learn to prepare the paint or other medium. This preparation becomes a great experience to promote the children's self-esteem—and it enhances your own professional growth as you realize the degree to which you have empowered them.

PRESENTING THE MATERIALS

Materials should be attractively laid out. Art supplies should not be kept in torn, unpainted cartons. These supplies are *not* waste materials and they should not be treated as such. It is more conducive to the creative use of art media if the materials are in attractive containers, such as the following:

- painted boxes,
- colorful trays,
- plastic carryalls,
- colored baskets,
- disposable aluminum foil baking pans,
- wooden boxes constructed especially for such use, and
- gift boxes.

For liquid media, use
- transparent plastic containers,
- commercial plastic paint containers with lids, and
- empty food cans that have been primed with an enamel undercoat and then enameled in various colors—one for each color of paint that is most ordinarily used. (Several cans may be primed for seasonal or unusual colors introduced later in the year.)

Six-ounce tomato paste cans are an excellent size for small hands to hold, yet they are balanced so that long-handled brushes will not tip them over. They are also especially good for toddlers using shorter brushes. Because the cans are small, they prevent the problem of having too much paint at one time.

When using such materials as metal lids or cardboard egg cartons in various art projects, have the older children paint them beforehand so that the containers are inviting to use. Do not try to paint plastic containers. They can be decorated with marking pens, however.

Backgrounds

When materials are placed directly on the table, set them on a contrasting background to keep them visually, if not physically, within comfortable boundaries. Large sheets of cardboard or paper as well as trays of all kinds can be used as boundary keepers to help the materials appear organized and attractive. Lazy susans (turntables) are excellent to use. (See photos, pp. 1 and 163.)

More Containers

Muffin tins and egg cartons are frequently used as containers to separate collage materials and to hold small amounts of tempera paints, especially for color-mixing projects.

The sturdy white plastic containers that some restaurants receive pastry in are also very useful for keeping materials separated. Most plastic containers found in food markets are too flimsy, but keep your eyes open for ones that are stronger than ordinary.

Be on the alert for aluminum or plastic containers in which frozen foods and other products are packaged. You may not be familiar with all of the new packages on the market, but parents are usually very cooperative in letting you know about them and even collecting containers for your use.

Junior-size baby food jars, with lids, make excellent paint containers.

Be sure to provide a variety of containers, and change them occasionally so that the children learn to be flexible in their own choice of materials.

Accessibility

Materials should be readily accessible. Arrange the working area in such a way that the materials can be easily reached by the children who will be using them.

The materials do not necessarily need always to be placed right next to the child, however. *Movement* is important in all areas of growth. Art is the direct result of certain kinds of movement. Having to move to nearby areas to obtain needed materials and carry them back to the working area helps children to establish generalized motor patterns within their physiological systems. (For more information about the value of movement for young children, see Cherry, *Creative Movement for the Developing Child,* Fearon Teacher Aids, 1971, and Cherry, Godwin, and Staples, *Is the Left Brain Always Right?* Fearon Teacher Aids, 1989.)

CHAPTER 2

Paper

Lorraine's grandmother came to visit. She was very much interested in the child's nursery school, and began to question her about it. Four-year-old Lorraine, quickly becoming impatient with the cross-examination, said with finality, "Oh, you know. School is where they give you lots of paper to write on."

We take paper so much for granted that we often fail to notice the thrill with which children react to this great motivational material. From neat piles of colored paper on shelves, from large rolls of newsprint or butcher paper in closets, from boxes of scraps and remnants, and from piles of old newspapers stacked high—from all these kinds of paper come hints of exciting projects and the chance to explore art media, tools, and ideas.

HOW TO SELECT PAPER

Lack of funds should not keep you from having a good supply of paper, because there are many free or inexpensive kinds of paper available. By knowing the characteristics of various types of paper, you can put available funds to good use.

Paper is generally judged by its weight, texture, strength, color, thickness, and opaqueness. The most expensive kinds are made from cloth rags. Most paper we buy today, however, has little rag content or none at all. It is made with wood pulp instead. The greater the wood pulp content, the more quickly the paper will become brittle and yellowed. Although wood pulp paper is cheaper than paper with a high rag content, occasionally have the children take something home that is on this longer-lasting paper so that in years to come parents can have the thrill of rediscovering the early art work of their children without finding that it has crumbled to pieces.

Let your students use many different kinds of paper. The suitability of some particular kind is of little importance to young children. What is important is the subtle cumulative learning about the differences in texture, absorbency, permanency, transparency, sturdiness, and attractiveness of various papers. If the teacher plans ahead of time to change the methods of presenting the projects—to change the shapes, colors, and textures of the paper—each new art activity can be an adventure to the children, and each new type of paper will reinforce what they learned from other types.

GENERAL PAPER SUPPLY

Manila Paper. This commonly used paper is inexpensive and satisfactory for both painting and drawing. It becomes brittle with age, however, so do not stock manila paper too far in advance. If you use it extensively, substitute paper of more lasting quality from time to time.

White Drawing Paper. Available in many qualities and weights, this is the best all-round type of paper to use if your budget can afford it. The 60-lb. weight is adequate for general use, and the 80-lb. weight is excellent. They both take paint well and are good for cutting, crayoning, pasting, folding, and similar activities.

Mill Screening Paper. Sometimes called oatmeal paper or Roughtex, this paper is notable for its textural quality; mill screening paper is especially good to use with crayons and chalks and for print making. It is available in colors, but it is most commonly used in natural or buff.

Construction Paper. This smooth-surfaced, colored paper is usually obtainable in 80-lb. or 85-lb. weights. It is excellent for general art work.

Poster Paper. This is similar to construction paper, but it is lighter—usually approximately 40-lb. weight. Poster paper is easier for the 2- or 3-year-old to fold and cut than construction paper.

Fadeless Art Paper. Though light in weight, this paper is durable and strong in color, making it suitable for many art activities. It costs slightly more than construction paper, but its resistance to fading makes it well worth the higher cost. It is very easy to fold and cut, and it is especially good for displays. Only one side is colored; the other is white.

Butcher Paper, Wrapping Paper, and Freezer Paper. These kinds of papers can be purchased in rolls from paper supply houses or wholesale grocery outlets. Butcher paper is especially good for fingerpainting, but it can also be used for all other types of art activities. Try to obtain 30- or 36-inch-wide rolls, which will give you much flexibility in the sizes you can cut it into. Brown wrapping paper is especially good as background paper for murals and for oversized drawings and paintings. The brown background emphasizes color and design that might otherwise be overwhelmed on stark white paper.

Coated Fingerpaint Paper. Buy this only if it is of excellent quality. Otherwise, substitute other papers.

Oak Tagboard or Index Bristol. Tagboard is inexpensive cardboard, light enough in weight for use in making booklets, greeting cards, folders, and similar items.

Newsprint. This is available as end rolls from newspaper companies or from educational supply companies. I prefer colored newsprint because the color seems to give the paper more body.

SUPPLEMENTARY PAPER

You may wish to supplement your basic paper supply with odds and ends of all kinds of papers, such as the following:

Cardboard from food packages	Gummed colored paper
Colored tissue	Gummed crepe paper
Computer paper	Japanese rice paper
Con-Tact paper	Paper plates
Corrugated paper	Parchment
Crepe paper	Place mats
Doilies	Sandpaper
Duplicator paper	Tracing paper
Facial tissues	Typing paper
Fluorescent papers	Velour
Gift-wrapping paper	Watercolor paper

IMAGINATION PAPER

Imagination paper is just what the name suggests. You use your imagination to stimulate the children's imaginations

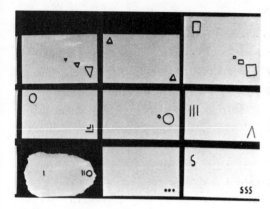

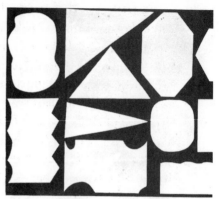

Here are a few pieces of Imagination Paper.

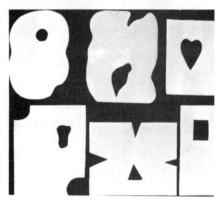

And here are some samples of what 4- and 5-year-olds can do with it.

when they use the paper. For example, cut sheets of paper in geometrical shapes. Make circles. Make squares. Cut triangular shapes. Cut long, narrow pieces and short, fat pieces. Cut free forms and five-sided or six-sided pieces. Sometimes you can make negative-space imagination paper. Cut circles, free-form shapes, and other designs into the paper. Cut large and small holes, balanced and unbalanced designs. Let your imagination be your guide. You can also put marks on the paper. Mark it with a B or an A or even a Z. Mark it with one dot or two or perhaps three in a row. Make a triangle in one corner and a cross in another. Make two little squares right in the center of the paper. Make the marks with pen, paint, or crayon. Make them big or very small. Make them fat or narrow. However you mark the paper, mark it with imagination.

Use this special paper for any creative developmental art projects. Present it with no special comments about its size, shape, or markings. Let the children discover for themselves. Let them cope with the special problems that your imagination may have created for them, and give them the freedom to put their own imaginations to work.

THE SCRAP BOX

If you're like me, you'll have a dozen scrap boxes filled with a priceless collection of odds and ends. We put all paper scraps accumulated during cutting activities into our scrap boxes. Whenever anyone uses the scissors, every scrap of paper is saved for future pasting, cutting, and decorating experiences. This year we may be using a box of scraps accumulated two or three years ago. Out of it come the bits and pieces of long-forgotten projects, surprising us with their exciting colors, designs, textures, and shapes.

SIZES

Just as you vary the shapes and kinds of paper, you should vary the sizes. Although the children require opportunities to use their large muscles, and therefore respond well to very large pieces of paper, you should challenge their abilities with many different sizes of paper. Proportions, too, should be varied.

STORAGE

Give careful consideration to storing your paper. Store it in such a way that you can get to it easily when you need it. Keep the different kinds separated. Always have sufficient quantities readily available for use.

If you don't have shelves that are large enough to store large pieces of paper, make portfolios out of the sides of cardboard cartons. Store each type of paper in a separate portfolio. Or use a very large carton as a paper-storage file. To help keep different sizes of paper separated from one another in a limited amount of shelf space, stack the paper flat, storing each size in a flat cardboard gift box. Another way to store large paper is to make a number of narrow shelves on an existing shelf by stacking plywood boards with blocks of wood, shallow boxes, or bricks between them.

If you can't find room for very large pieces of paper, simply roll them up. If you have a storage room, save most of your paper there, keeping only small quantities of paper on hand in the classroom. This arrangement prevents unnecessary handling of the paper.

PAPER SHAPES THROUGH THE YEAR

Concepts can be reinforced and motivation stimulated by varying not only the types and sizes of paper used in art activities, but the shapes of the paper as well. You can use the following schedule as a guide and as a basis for your own ideas throughout the year.

September. Throughout this month the children should be encouraged to explore, use, observe, and experience round and circular shapes and forms.

Start with circular shapes. The children enjoy round paper for painting, coloring, cutting, and pasting because there are no difficult corners to cope with.

- Offer round paper with crayons and paint.
- Use round paper for the first cutting experiences.
- Small paper circles can be pasted on larger circles.
- Create bulletin board displays with circular backgrounds.
- Display round objects in front of the displays.
- Also, place round objects in your mystery boxes for feeling and touching experiences.

Allow the children to discover the concept of roundness on their own; you don't have to explain it. Yet, one day, when you ask the children to sit in a circle, each child will know exactly what you mean.

October. Introduce rectangular shapes.

Ask the children, preferably in small groups of three or four, "What is different about this paper?" Help them discover that rectangular shapes have corners. Reinforce this discovery by finding the corners of objects and by walking to the corners of the room.

As the end of the month approaches, return to circular shapes. Present the appropriate colors of paint and watch the children turn these shapes into pumpkins and other Halloween designs.

November. Pasting, painting, and coloring activities take on a new dimension with the introduction of pennant-shaped paper. Because the children will usually make use of the wide end of the paper first, placing that end at their left will encourage a left-to-right progression of arm movements.

Pasting cutouts on pennant shapes provides vital learning experiences in seriation (see photos on p. 17).

Help the children discover that the pennants have points. Pennant shapes can be varied to form leaf shapes, perhaps with many points. Provide the appropriate colors of paint and crayons, and the children will produce beautiful fall-oriented designs.

Return to round shapes again by drawing circles on bright colors of construction paper for cutting. The resultant fruit shapes can be used for Thanksgiving decorations.

December. Introduce triangles.

Provide the appropriate colors of paint or crayons together with triangular-shaped paper. Then watch the children create beautiful Christmas tree designs.

Triangular shapes may also be offered with scissors and paste.

January. Introduce square-shaped paper. Squares are easy— no surprises, no narrow corners.

- A square is the same length on each side.
- A square fits into a circle.
- A circle fits into a square.
- A square can be folded diagonally to form two equal triangles.
- Joining two squares makes one long rectangle.

Square paper provides an interesting change from the rectangular-shaped paper used for most art activities.

Decorate the room with snowflakes. Have the children help you make cone shapes from square pieces of thin paper and then cut designs into them.

February. Folding activities can be continued by folding squares or rectangles over once for cutting heart-shaped designs. The children may decorate these with paint, crayons, or collage materials.

March. Introduce diamond-shaped paper in time for the kite-flying season. (This shape may be used again in May for the Japanese kite holiday.)

Diamond shapes are difficult for young children to comprehend. Try comparing them to squares standing on end.

April. Oval-shaped paper, decorated with strips of precut ribbons and other trimmings, may be used to make beautiful giant Easter eggs.

May. Scalloped circular shapes of paper may motivate the children to make flower designs, which can be used for Mother's Day decorations and gifts.

This shape also works well for Cinco de Mayo designs.

June. Experienced children will enjoy working with others in making murals on long sheets of wrapping or butcher paper spread out on the floor. These can be decorated with paints, crayons, chalks, collage materials, or a combination of all.

July. If it is a hot day, let the children draw or paint on oversized sheets of paper in a variety of shapes on the floor, where it is cooler.

Provide the appropriate colors of paint and large, rectangular-shaped pieces of paper for patriotic paintings.

August. Have the children lie down on large sheets of paper so that you can trace the outlines of their bodies with pencil or crayon.

Let the children paint their outlines as they view themselves. The older children may wish to cut theirs out. After one year of creative art experiences, the paintings they produce will probably show a positive self-image.

The project can also be done by cutting out a second body shape, stapling the two shapes together around the edges, and stuffing the body with paper for a 3-D effect.

CHAPTER 3

Color

Color is magic. Color is the blue wooly sweater and the green-like-grass top. Color is melting butter on warm toast or sparkling gelatin on crispy lettuce. It's the lipstick Mama is wearing and it's Daddy's shiny brown shoes. It's the flower in the vase and the bicycle on the sidewalk. It's a kitten, soft and furry, and it is also a fish, glistening in the aquarium. Color is the rosy glow of the setting sun and the velvet sky as its shadows deepen with the darkening hour. Color is magic, readily available to all and free for use by young children. Experience color with them. Take them by the hands and plunge headlong into the very essence of color's feelings and color's effects. You can afford to be generous. Dish color out in liberal portions and let the children know that it thrills you. Share with them color's sparkle and gloss, color's quietness and music, color's smell and touch. And watch the children grow.

THE IMPORTANCE OF COLORS AS CUES

Color is the cue by which we determine the quality of a shape. Although the shape may take precedence in defining what a thing is, color more deeply touches our innermost feelings. Young children between 3 and 5 years of age, with normal perceptual development, are more concerned with the colors of objects than with their shapes. Before the age of 3, children are dependent upon tactile cues. They are motivated by whether or not they can grasp a thing, not by what color it is. They need to touch the thing with the entire hand to find out how it feels, how it is shaped, and what it does. As children become more socially oriented, however, and more aware of their own self and their own feelings and moods, they are more open to the impressionable effect of color.

COLOR IS NOT ABSOLUTE

Although shape and form are absolute, color is not. A ball is round in any light, though it may appear to be distorted by certain light effects. A square block in the toy box is square on each of its six sides, whether the block is barely visible in dim light or strongly evident in bright sunshine. Color, however, does not remain constant. The slightest change in light will affect it. Color varies according to the amount, intensity, and type of light under which it is perceived. A color looks different in the morning sun and in the soft light of a foggy day. It looks different under a fluorescent lamp and under the light of an incandescent bulb. Each individual interprets the wavelengths that produce color in his or her own unique way. For our purpose here, we don't need to understand how light waves are interpreted by the human brain as color, but some simple experiments can pave the way for a deeper appreciation of the excitement and vitality of this magic called color.

COLOR PRINCIPLES

A goal-directed program of color awareness and self-discovery will help young children become more aware of their own natural instinct for color harmony. In order to set the stage for such a program, you should have a working knowledge of some of the basic terminology of color and color harmony. Some definitions you should know are listed below.

Hue. A color in its purest form. This term also applies to black, white, gray, and brown.

Primary Colors. *Red, blue,* and *yellow* are the *primary* colors and form the basis for the color wheel (see p. 60). All other colors are a result of some mixture of these colors.

Secondary Colors. *Orange, green,* and *violet* are the *secondary* colors. They are made by mixing equal parts of any two of the three primary colors. A simple color wheel can be made by using the three primary and the three secondary colors. All other colors on the color wheel are variations of these.

Complementary Colors. *Colors that are opposite each other* on the color wheel are *complementary*. Two colors that are complementary will make *brown* when mixed. Therefore, brown goes well with any complementary pair. Only one pair of complementary colors should be used in an art project. Two pairs will cancel each other out.

Split-complementary. When *one color of a complementary pair* on a color wheel *is replaced by the two colors on each side of it,* the three colors then make up a *split-complementary.* Split-complementaries are easier to harmonize with one another than are pure complementaries.

Warm and Cold. In general, the colors from *the yellows through the reds* are considered to be *warm.* Colors from *the greens through the blues and violets* are considered to be *cold.* The warm colors have a tendency to come *forward;* the cold colors seem to *recede.* All colors are also affected by their tints and shades; the darker tones seem to recede, and the lighter tones seem to be larger and closer.

Intensity. *Pure colors are the most intense.* Colors are less intense if they contain black, white, or their complementary color.

Tone or Value. These terms refer to *how dark or how light a color is.* To darken or reduce the value of high-intensity colors, such as yellow or orange, add black. To increase the value of low-intensity colors, such as violet or blue, add a small amount of white. Too much white, however, will make the color a tint.

Tints and Shades. Colors to which *white* has been added are called *tints.* Colors to which *black or their complements* have been added are called *shades.* The shade of a color can also be varied by adding a small quantity of an analogous color.

Analogous Colors. Colors that are found *next to each other on the color wheel* are called *analogous.* They are also called related colors.

COLOR EXPERIMENTS AND EXPERIENCES

COLOR MAGIC
This activity demonstrates how colors change when they are mixed with each other.

Materials
6 clear plastic drinking glasses for each child
Water
Red, blue, and yellow tempera paint

Procedure

Fill each glass half full of water.

Tell the children to put a few drops of red tempera paint in one of their glasses, a few drops of blue in another, and a few drops of yellow in a third. They can then make orange by pouring a little of the red water and the yellow water into another glass. They can make green by mixing the blue and the yellow. Depending upon the children's interest in the activity, you can give them additional glasses and let them experiment further with mixing various colors.

Variations

- After the children have worked with straight color, give them some white paint so that they can experiment with intensity changes.
- If you prefer, this activity can be done with food coloring or with watercolor paints. If you use food coloring, try to get the kind used by bakeries because it has the widest range of colors and intensities. Plastic eyedroppers are good to use for measuring out the food coloring. They are available from surgical supply houses.

COLOR PADDLES

Whether commercially purchased or homemade, color paddles can bring the magic of color directly under children's visual control. Here's how to make your own color paddles.

Materials

3" x 3" squares of cardboard or tagboard
Red, yellow, and blue cellophane
Ice cream sticks or tongue depressors
Glue or stapler

Procedure

For each color paddle, cut the centers out of two 3-inch-square pieces of cardboard. Cover the hole in one piece with colored cellophane. Attach an ice cream stick or tongue depressor to use as a handle. Put the two pieces of cardboard together and attach them with glue or staples. The cellophane and one end of the handle should be between the two cardboard squares. Your color paddle is now complete.

Make three paddles: one with red, one with yellow, and one with blue cellophane. You may have to use two layers of the cellophane, depending on the brand, to make a strong enough color.

Have the children experiment looking through the color paddles one at a time and also through different combinations.

SUNSHINE WINDOWS

On gloomy, bleak days, when the sun has been hiding for too long, the children can still face the world with "sunshine."

Materials
    Small paper plates
    Yellow cellophane
    Ice cream sticks or tongue depressors
    Glue or staples

Procedure
Make the frame for a Sunshine Window by cutting the middle out of a small paper plate. Cover the opening with yellow cellophane, and attach a handle. The children hold the plates in front of their eyes and look through the cellophane.

Variation
• The same idea can be used to make "sunglasses" out of tagboard or paper plates.

COLOR WHEEL

Make an oversized color wheel following the directions on page 60. Have the children locate on the color wheel the colors of objects in the room.

COLOR WALK

Go for a walk specifically to look for colors. How many different kinds of green can you see? Compare the colors of roofs. Collect samples of bark from trees and compare their colors. Find something that is red. Find something that matches someone's sweater. What color is the sky? The street? The sidewalk?

AUTUMN LEAVES

Collect as many different colors of autumn leaves as possible and use them for displays and collage projects.

STAINED GLASS WINDOWS

To prepare for this activity, visit buildings where there are stained glass windows.

Materials
    Cellophane in several colors
    Cellophane tape or glue (or you may be able to make the
       cellophane stick to the window glass with static electricity)
    Black plastic tape (optional)

Procedure
Decorate a portion of a window in the classroom with colored cellophane to duplicate the effect of stained glass. (Use a window that will receive direct sunshine at some time during the day.) For more realistic stained glass, use black plastic tape to outline the cellophane as you fasten the various pieces to the window.

Variation

• You might cover an entire window with one color or with strips of red, blue, and yellow.

PAINT CHIPS

Get duplicate sets of color chips from the paint store. Paste one set on cardboard. Have the children match the colors with chips from the other set.

COLOR GAME

For an active experience with a group of children, play "Police Officer, I've Lost My Child."

Teacher: Police officer, I've lost my little girl.
Child: What was she wearing?
Teacher: She was wearing a green and yellow dress.
Child: Here she is.

The child who is "found" then becomes the police officer and identifies the next "lost" child by the color of a piece of clothing he or she is wearing.

COLORED LIGHTS

Materials

Flashlight
Various colors of cellophane
Tape or rubber bands
Record player and records

Procedure

Cover the ends of several flashlights with different colors of cellophane. You may need more than one layer to produce strongly enough colored light.

Melted Crayons.

In a darkened room, experiment with the colors of the various lights as they interact with one another. Play music during this activity.

Variation
• The flashlight glass can be colored with transparent water-color, colored inks, or felt-tip marking pens. An even better effect can be obtained by coloring the bulbs or using colored bulbs.

MELTED CRAYONS
Drawing with warm crayons produces translucent colors. Held up to a window, the paper has the brilliance of stained glass.

Materials
>Electric food-warming tray
>A box of peeled kindergarten-sized crayons
>Paper
>Thick block of wood

Procedure

Place the food-warming tray at the front right corner of a low table. Adjust the heat to medium.

The children each in turn place a piece of paper on the tray. They can use a block of wood in one hand to hold down the paper. When they rub the crayons over the paper on the warm tray, the crayons will rapidly melt, producing smears, blotches, and spots of transparent colored wax.

Variation

- Try drawing on many different types of paper, including waxed paper, aluminum foil, and typing paper. Each kind produces a different effect.

MARBLE ROLLS

This interesting color experiment uses marbles.

Materials
>Several small dishes of
>   different colors of paint
>Several marbles for each
>   dish
>Cardboard box
>Sheets of paper the size of
>   the bottom of the box
>Teaspoons

Marble Rolls.

Procedure

Place a sheet of paper inside the bottom of the box. The child uses a teaspoon to take a painted marble out of one of the dishes. He or she drops the marble into the box and moves the box back and forth and side to side, noting the colored lines formed by the paint coming off the marble. This process can then be repeated with marbles in other colors of paint.

COLOR GUIDE THROUGH THE YEAR

Use this basic color guide to develop a plan to increase the children's color awareness. Don't try to use every color combination here in any one year, but use them as the taking-off point for your own ideas. Refer to this guide when planning what basic colors of tempera to make available, what crayons to use, and what colors of paper to provide. Intersperse these various ideas with general selections of colors. Start using the guide in September.

1. Red, blue, yellow — Primary colors only.
2. Red and blue only
3. Yellow and blue only — Mix these colors to make green. Compare with leaves, grass, flower stems. Be sure to do this before all greens fade into autumn colors.
4. Yellow, blue, green
5. Red and yellow only — Discuss resultant orange. Compare with the colors of citrus fruits—oranges, lemons, tangerines.
6. Yellow and orange — Halloween is approaching.
7. Orange and black — Use orange paint on black paper or black on orange.
8. Orange, black, white — Vary colors as above.

9. Yellow orange, orange, red orange, yellow	Compare with the colors of raw and cooked pumpkin.
10. Red, orange, yellow, green	Use on brown paper for an autumn effect.
11. Brown, yellow, red orange	Autumn-leaves effect.
12. Orange, green, violet	Secondary colors only.
13. Orange, green, violet, red, blue, yellow	Primary and secondary colors.
14. Red and green	Christmas is approaching.
15. Red, green, blue	
16. Dark green, bright green, dark red, bright red	Also for Christmas.
17. Magenta and yellow green	A unique Christmas combination. Can also be used for Chanukah.
18. Blue and orange	It's Chanukah time, too.
19. Turquoise blue and orange	
20. Two or three shades of blue plus white	Also for Chanukah.
21. Blue, green, magenta, white	Use on black paper.
22. Complementary colors	Use only one pair at a time, with black and white, or brown and white.
23. Analogous colors: Red, magenta, red orange, orange; blue, blue green, green, yellow green; green, yellow green, orange, yellow orange; violet, magenta, blue violet, blue	Rainy days bring plenty of time to experiment.
24. White	Use on black paper on a snowy day.
25. White and black	Use on blue paper on a foggy day.
26. Red, white, blue	February brings patriotic holidays.

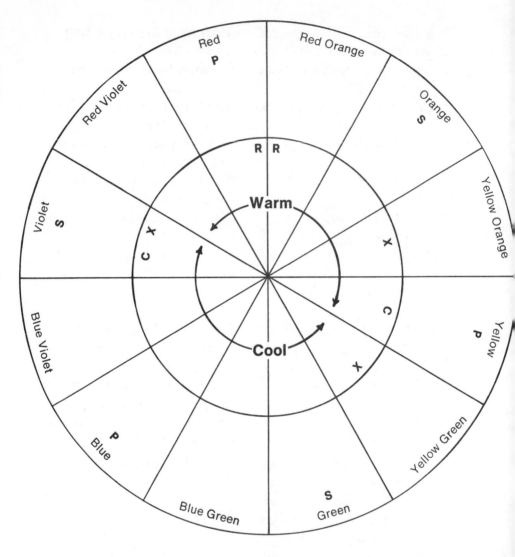

Color wheel. Using transparent watercolors, crayons, or oil pastels, you can make your own color wheel on this form by following these simple directions. Put each primary and secondary color in its own space in the outer ring of the circle *and* in the space to either side of it. The overlapping colors in every other space will form combination colors: red violet, red orange, yellow green, blue green, and blue violet. (Blue violet is very difficult for young children to distinguish from blue. Do not expect them to be able to.)

Key

P Primary color
S Secondary color
R Related color
C Complementary color
X Split-complementary

27. Red, pink, white	Valentine's Day is coming.
28. Red, pink, white, light blue	
29. Red, magenta, pink, light blue	Unusual Valentine colors.
30. White with primary colors	Add the white to each color experimentally.
31. Black with primary colors	Add the black to each color experimentally.
32. Black and white with primary colors	Add the black and white experimentally.
33. White with secondary colors	Add the white to each color experimentally.
34. Black with secondary colors	Add the black to each color experimentally.
35. Several pastel tints of *one* color	
36. Several shaded pastel tints of *one* color	Made by adding minute quantities of black to pastel tints.
37. Six different pastel colors	Spring is here.
38. Red, white, green	Cinco de Mayo. These are the colors of the Mexican flag.
39. All colors, including some tints and shades	Provide 12 to 15 different colors from which the children may select their paints.
40. Red, white, blue	4th of July.

CHAPTER 4

Crayons

The waxy smell of the rub-it-until-it's-shiny crayon! The smoothness of the waxed-over surface! The thrill of getting a brand new box of crayons and trying out each color! The delicate shadings of the rub-it-lightly-like-Mama-does picture! The scribbles and the scribble picture! And the exciting sheets of paper where the crayons leave their beautiful marks.

Few materials are as familiar to the average adult as crayons and paper, which most of us remember from our own early childhoods. Few materials have been used so universally in all areas of public elementary education. And few materials have been used so extensively in all areas of art activity and at all levels of development. Yet we find the importance of crayons is frequently minimized, and they are treated rather lightly in many art books. In fact, crayons are wonderful tools for art at any level, but they are ideal for children's beginning scribbles and their first explorations into creativity. Crayons are inexpensive and long lasting, so it is easy to have them around. For children, they are easy to manipulate and control. The many things the children do with them lead to an enhancement of creative thinking and development.

Crayons are important in the development of writing skills. Children can practice moving their arms, wrists, palms, and fingers as they push crayons back and forth and round and round. At first the movements are random, jerky, and uncertain. Gradually, a sense of coordination sets in and a rhythmic movement is developed. This prepares children for writing, where similar, but more purposeful, motions are necessary.

Crayons are also important in developing figure-ground discrimination, symbol formation, and symbol recognition. Although children make similar movements when they use paintbrushes and paint, the symbols children make with a brush are usually less distinguishable to them than the finer-lined drawings made with a crayon. Whereas brush painting employs a great deal of shoulder and arm movement, crayoning depends more on wrist, hand, and finger movements.

Crayons are dependable and readily available. Unlike paints, they don't need water or refilling or brushes or adult assistance. Children can get them from a cupboard or off a shelf and, without any help from anyone, use them. Although children

Large kindergarten-sized crayons and a long roll of paper provide endless fascination for David (4). Placing the paper on his right encourages him to work from left to right in preparation for future writing experiences.

may need to be reminded that walls and furniture are not for drawing on—that crayons are to be used only on paper or other specially provided materials—they can use crayons independently. Being able to make something on one's own is an important ego developer and helps to build self-esteem.

Crayons are important because of their beautiful colors and because of the exciting world they help children bring within the realm of their own control. Crayons make the sun yellow, the grass green, and the flowers blue and purple and red. They can make rosy cheeks and smoking chimneys. They can make rainbows.

Crayons are also important because they can be used to express feelings and satisfy emotions. Even 2-year-olds can experience the thrill of the kinesthetic sensations that their scribbles produce within their bodies, the smell of the crayon's wax, and the faint sound of the crayon being rubbed to and fro on a piece of paper.

Crayons, the ABC of art, should always be presented to children with excitement and care. They should be stored where children can get them at will. They should be kept in small, sturdy, neat containers from which they can be grabbed easily, rather than in the tuck-in boxes out of which they must be shaken. Crayons should be kept in groups of selected colors, rather than allowed to get all mixed up so that one box doesn't have any red or green, and another box seems to have all the blacks and purples, and no one knows what happened to the oranges and yellows.

SIZES OF CRAYONS

Very young children should be given thick crayons that they can grasp with the entire hand. Some crayons are made with a knob at one end to make them easy to grasp. But these are made of a type of plastic that does not have the tactile quality of wax crayons. They should be used only long enough to teach toddlers not to put crayons in their mouths and to make marks only on the surface provided. The short, stubby crayons now put out by several manufacturers are comfortable for toddlers to grasp and can be used for children through at least 3 years of age. Four- and five-year-olds will do better with kindergarten-sized crayons. These come in a number of styles and varying thicknesses from the different manufacturers. Any thick, good-quality crayon will do as long as it is waxy, yet hard enough to resist breaking. Some people prefer nonroll crayons because they stay where they are placed on a table top, giving children more control over them.

Along with the large crayons, a selection of regular-sized crayons of many colors may be made available for occasional experimentation. Regular crayons will break, however, and young children tire more easily when using them. But the children should find this out for themselves and have the opportunity to try out regular crayons to verify their progress from time to time. When the children are ready for more delicate fine motor movements and have increased control of the muscles in their fingers, they are ready to use the regular-sized crayons. By the time most children are approximately 5½ years of age, they have developed sufficient fine-motor control of their hands and fingers to enable them to achieve dependable fingertip control.

QUALITY OF CRAYONS

Do not assume that all brands of crayons are alike. Before ordering large quantities of any crayon, sample several brands. Then make your choice according to brightness of color, balance of wax and color, sturdiness, whether it smears easily, and how the colors blend with one another. When you have decided which brand you are most comfortable with, you can be fairly certain that it is probably the best brand to use for

Lab

ege of Education Health & Human Services

University of Michigan-Dearborn

children, even though it may cost slightly more than a brand that seemed too waxy or whose colors seemed to clash with one another.

PRESENTING THE CRAYONS

Sometimes children should each be given their own container of six or eight colors. They should always be encouraged to keep the crayons to the left of the paper, since this is the side they will eventually start writing from. Some days they should be asked to share their supply with others. Then all the crayons can be mixed together in one container within equal reach of all the sharers. Selecting crayons from the middle of a table calls for a different type of hand-eye movement than that used when a set of crayons is beside each child's paper.

One of the positive qualities of crayons is that they last a long time. Even so, bring out a new supply once in a while for the aesthetic effect of the unblemished colors.

CONTAINERS

Crayons in lift-lid boxes may be kept in the boxes for use. If you get them by bulk or in tuck-in boxes, it's best to provide other neat, colorful containers. I have used painted cigar boxes, colorful plastic boxes and baskets, and small reed baskets.

DARK-COLORED VS. LIGHT-COLORED CRAYONS

You can teach the children that dark-colored crayons are sometimes softer than light ones because dark crayons contain more wax, which makes them opaque. (This tendency is most noticeable in less expensive brands.) When dark colors are used over lighter paper or lighter colors of crayon, the colors underneath won't show through. Because they contain less wax, lighter-colored crayons are harder than dark ones. This hardness keeps the lighter-colored crayons from adhering heavily to the surface they are covering, so they will give a more transparent color than the dark ones. Consequently, light crayons can produce a third color when they are used on colored paper or over another light crayon color. For the best results, suggest to the children that they try not to press too hard with the crayons. The less wax that comes off, the greater the transparency.

PEELED CRAYONS

You may want to keep a supply of peeled crayons to be rubbed sideways over the paper. You can also supply peeled crayons that you have notched on the edges. These can be used to create special designs from time to time. I have found it best to cut no more than four notches in a crayon. More than that seems to become too confusing and the crayon does not make the best looking designs. The short, stubby toddler crayons are good for cutting notches into, and they can be used by people of all ages.

BLACK CRAYONS

Keep a separate supply of black crayons to give to children from time to time for outlining paper collages, especially when they have been working with cutouts of geometric shapes. At the age of 2, children will usually scribble over the collage with the crayons. As their perceptual powers develop, they will gradually begin making vague outlines around some of the shapes.

Geometric shapes outlined in black crayon by a 4½-year-old.

Eventually, children will clearly emphasize the geometric shapes with the black crayon. They may even attempt to copy some of the shapes elsewhere on the paper. These are all natural processes, and you do not have to give directions for outlining. Simply provide the crayons as the children finish their collages.

Occasionally you can give 4- and 5-year-olds black crayons to outline the colors in their tempera paintings. This will increase their awareness of how they are utilizing space and color. Older children especially enjoy creating such designs over their more complex paintings.

FLUORESCENT CRAYONS

Crayons are now available in lovely fluorescent colors. The colors are not very brilliant, and children are sometimes disappointed in their lack of emphasis. They are very good to experiment with, however, in order to find out what they can and cannot do. These crayons work best on a good drawing paper, to which they will adhere more easily than to a smooth paper. The colors show up best on a white background, since they are somewhat more transparent than the traditional crayons.

PSYCHEDELIC EFFECT

You can achieve psychedelic effects by using a pair of complementary colors, as shown on the color wheel on page 60. Any complementary pair will give a striking effect. If you combine two pairs of complementary colors, they will cancel each other out and cause a feeling of discord. You will lose the psychedelic effect.

VARIETY CRAYONS

Many varieties of crayons are available today: the fluorescent colors mentioned above, multicolored sticks with several colors parallel to one another, and multicolored blocks with bits of different colors pressed together so that a different color comes onto the paper with each stroke. There are also plastic crayons, which, like the knobbed crayons already mentioned, do not have the tactile effect of the wax. Older children might like them for creating special drawing effects, but I don't recommend them for preschool children. Whatever unique types of crayons you may find, remember to use them only for occasional novelty. Children do not always need a gimmick. Their creativity and their development will be promoted through familiarity, gained through practice, with one particular type of crayon.

Experimenting with new materials is a fine way to explore possibilities and to instill in children a sense of scientific awareness. However, your basic goals should be to encourage the development of creativity through crayons and to provide children with inspiration to pursue their creative urges through the use of common materials.

SCRIBBLE COOKIES

Save the stub ends of old crayons to make scribble cookies. Simply peel all the paper off the crayons. Separate them by color and break them into very small pieces. Put the pieces of each color into a separate section of a muffin pan. Place the pan in a warm oven with the heat *turned off* and let the crayons melt slowly. When they are fully melted, remove the pan from the oven and let it cool. You will end up with Scribble Cookies— bright, shiny, and new. Children can grasp them with their entire hand. They are great for rubbing, scribbling, and general experimentation. Since the temptation to bite into these enticing cookies is sometimes overwhelming, toddlers need to be reminded that they are not for eating.

Another way to melt crayons is to heat them with a light bulb. Place a light bulb connected to an electric cord inside a box that has an opening in the top just large enough to hold the muffin tin. (You'll need to make a hole in the side of the box for the cord to go through. It is also a good idea to rest the bulb on a metal pan to prevent scorching the box.) Plug in the light bulb and watch the crayons melt. This can be developed as a science project in which the children participate.

Crayons can also be melted by putting the muffin tin in a pan of boiling water. This is easier but not as much fun as melting them over a light bulb. Commercial kits for the renewal of old crayons are also available through educational supply stores.

PAPER FOR CRAYONS

You can offer inexpensive newsprint or fine white drawing paper because almost any kind of paper is satisfactory for use with crayons, except paper with a very slick surface. The paper's surface needs to be of a kind to which the wax will adhere; thus, rough-textured papers are especially interesting.

Brown wrapping paper has a good texture for crayons and is often a welcome and educational contrast to the traditional white paper children are used to having.

Construction paper has an excellent surface for drawing on, but because it is quite expensive, it should be supplemented with less costly types of paper. If you do use construction paper, remember that the crayons are transparent and will be affected by the color of the paper. Generally, you should use the lighter colors of paper, except for special effects. However, the children can experiment and find out for themselves which crayon colors look best on the dark papers. (See "Color Changes," p. 78.)

If you use newsprint, the colored type has more body than the uncolored, making it easier to handle. And the pale pastel colors make lovely backgrounds for crayoning.

Not only should children have experiences with crayoning on many types of paper, but the shapes and sizes of paper should be varied as well, as suggested in "Paper Shapes Through the Year," pages 42–46. In addition to rectangular shapes, paper may be round, square, or triangular. It can be cut into free-form shapes or into specific geometric shapes. It can be torn around the edges or cut very smoothly. It can be very large or very small. Each new shape and each new size will promote the perceptual-motor development, and thus the cognitive development, of the child.

AVOIDING MODELS AND PATTERNS

In the activity suggestions that follow in this chapter (and throughout the book), models and patterns are generally avoided. Avoid telling children what to draw or how to draw it; there are so many things in their lives that have to be done in a specific way. If art is to be used as a means for expression and for free development of aesthetic values and creative thinking skills, children should be allowed to use the materials in their own way, without being required to follow a model or pattern that you have created for them. Your task is to stimulate their creativity by what you present and how you present it and to allow the children to develop their own modes of processing thought and learning various skills.

A WORD ABOUT COLORING BOOKS

As an author, educator, and art teacher, I have been frequently asked what I think of coloring books. Coloring books definitely have no place in your art curriculum. The biggest mistake in the use of coloring books, as in the use of patterns and diagrams to be colored, is that they too frequently take the place of creative endeavors. I tell parents not to feel guilty about providing their children with coloring books to use at home, however, as long as they

1. supplement the coloring books with plenty of blank sheets of good drawing paper,
2. let the children know they do not have to "stay within the lines,"
3. encourage them to use their imagination as to colors and color combinations, and
4. above all, purchase only books with really good drawings. So many coloring books have such poor art work that they

are a real disservice to the children to whom they are given. If you can't find a coloring book with good drawings, substitute a blank scrapbook instead, and tell the children to create their own coloring books.

In short, coloring books should be viewed as toys, rather than as a means of artistic expression.

The positive side of coloring books is that, for beginning readers and writers (at least 6 years of age), the task of staying within the lines is an excellent way to exercise eye-hand coordination skills.

For children of about 6 years of age and older, coloring books can be used with watercolors and a good-quality, fine-pointed paintbrush. The act of keeping the point of the brush within the corners of shapes is also excellent for increasing visual acuity and eye-hand coordination. It is especially beneficial to 7- to 9-year-olds who may be having reading or writing difficulties.

WHAT TO DO WITH CRAYONS

The main thing to do with crayons is to *make them available.* They should have a place on the toy shelf along with puzzles, manipulative toys, blocks, games, and other educational materials. Paper, too, should be readily available so that the children may use the crayons whenever there is a choice of activities.

Children should have many opportunities each week to simply scribble on different shapes, sizes, and types of papers—especially on large sheets of paper spread out on the floor or over a table. Only through the repeated practice of a particular movement can children acquire *meaningful* control of that movement. Various crayoning techniques can be introduced from time to time as a further means of experimenting with and exploring the medium. A few suggestions follow.

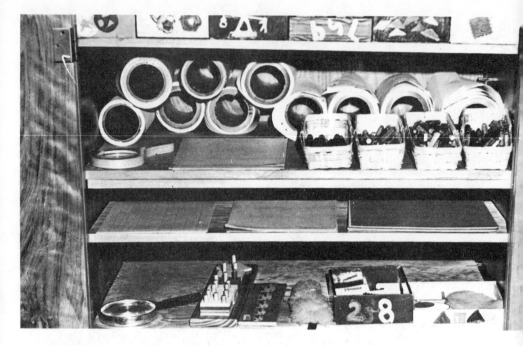

Baskets of crayons and plenty of paper are always available in this toy cupboard for children to use when they wish.

COLOR GUIDE THROUGH THE YEAR

For seasonal activities, follow the "Color Guide Through the Year" on pages 58–61 to vary the colors being used for special projects, thus enhancing the scope and variety of pictures produced by the children.

SCRIBBLE DESIGNS

Materials

12" x 18" sheets of drawing paper, newsprint, or comparable paper

Assortment of crayons (see the seasonal colors suggested on pp. 58–61 in "Color Guide Through the Year")

Procedure
Encourage children to scribble simple designs on paper.
Suggest that they fill in each space with a color.

Variations
• With a black crayon, outline a shape, using selected lines in the scribble design. Color in the spaces within the outlined area.
• Create people or animal shapes within the scribbles from the lines already made. Outline and fill in the spaces.
• Cut out around the outer edges of the scribble design. Paste the design on a contrasting color of construction paper.
• Fold the paper in half each way. Cut along the folds. Paste the four pieces on a sheet of construction paper slightly larger than the original paper. Suggest to the children that they match the corners of the scribble paper to the corners of the construction paper. The result will be the magical look of "Separated Scribbles."

Results
The advantage of doing scribble projects is that scribbling becomes more acceptable to the children, offsetting the remarks of people who feel all drawings must be representational. Finding shapes within the designs helps children to

1. *discriminate between sizes and forms of shapes,*
2. *relate abstract shapes to objects in real life,*
3. *improve their visual acuity as they search out and keep their eyes on the various spaces, lines, and the resultant shapes, and*
4. *improve muscular control as they adjust their movements to keep within the resultant spaces.*

Scribble projects are somewhat similar to coloring book activities, except that they are entirely the children's own creation and there is no right or wrong way to do them. (See pp. 74–75 for more on coloring books.)

MUSICAL DRAWINGS

Materials
    Large sheets of drawing paper
    Seasonal colors of crayons
    Musical accompaniment

Procedure
Children scribble to the sound of the music.

Results
Musical scribbling experiences help children to
    1. increase their rhythmic awareness,
    2. refine their auditory skills, and
    3. practice auditory-visual-motor coordination.
(See also "Arm Dancing," pp. 83–85.)

COLOR CHANGES

Materials
    Blue paper
    Yellow crayons

Procedure
Apply the yellow crayon to the blue paper to produce green lines or rubbings.

Variations
• Use *red* paper with white crayons to make pink, with yellow crayons to make orange, with blue crayons to make purple, and with green crayons to make brown.
• Use *blue* paper with white crayons to make light blue, with red crayons to make purple, with violet crayons to make blue violet, and with orange crayons to make brown.
• Use *green* paper with white crayons to make light green, with yellow crayons to make yellow green, and with blue crayons to make blue green.

• Allow the children to experiment with different selections of colors of paper and crayons.

• Encourage the children to try to achieve the same effects of color changes by rubbing one color over another on white paper. For the youngest children, use the sides of peeled crayons. Older children who have developed finer motor control can learn to achieve the same effects by applying a crayon very lightly to the paper.

Results

These experiments with the possibilities of color changes will

1. *give children an awareness of the versatility of crayons,*
2. *increase their knowledge of color relationships and the effect colors have on one another,*
3. *expand their awareness of transparency, and*
4. *give them a greater understanding of cause and effect and of their ability to control the materials by the colors they use.*

TEXTURED PAPERS

Materials

Sets of crayons with four to eight colors

Textured papers, approximately 9" x 12", such as charcoal paper, sandpaper, oatmeal paper, watercolor paper, paper towels, and corrugated paper

Procedure

Encourage children to try crayons on various papers to see what effects they will get.

Variations

Substitute other materials for the textured paper, such as

• pieces of wood with a rough finish,
• cement blocks or bricks,
• paper that the child has previously coated with tempera paint,

• textiles, and

• other textured materials that you may discover to use.

Results
Experimenting with crayons on textured surfaces will help children to

1. *classify materials according to texture,*
2. *develop muscular control as they find they must press very lightly on some materials to avoid tearing them,*
3. *discover the joy of experimentation, and*
4. *internalize ideas of the crayon's reaction to textured surfaces, which can be called on when applying other materials to textured surfaces.*

CRAYONS AND FINGERPAINTING

Materials
Fingerpaint paper, butcher paper, or a good quality art paper

Sets of crayons

Cups of fingerpaint

Pads of folded newspaper to put under the paper while crayoning

Procedure
Place newspaper pads under the paper. The pliable surface allows the crayons to be rubbed on heavily. Encourage children to scribble over the paper or to create a design if they prefer.

Cover the crayoned area with fingerpaint. The crayon design will show through.

Variations
• Use purple, blue, and green crayons with red or yellow paint.

• Use orange, yellow, and red crayons with blue or green paint.

• Use yellow, green, and black crayons with red or blue paint.

• Use one color of crayon and one color of fingerpaint.

- Use one color of crayon and two colors of fingerpaint.
- Use any of the crayon combinations above with two colors of paint.

Results
This exploration of fingerpainting over drawings may help children to
    1. *increase their sensitivity to colors and color combinations,*
    2. *become more aware of the possibilities of linear designs,*
    3. *become more conscious of their ability to control their muscular movements, and*
    4. *internalize their understanding of their ability to make changes through the use of color.*

SCRATCH BOARDS

This project requires a piece of paper or cardboard with an undercoating of crayon and an overcoating of another layer either of crayon or of paint. A design is then scratched into the top surface, allowing the crayoned layer on the bottom to show through. This is sometimes called *sgraffito,* an Italian term meaning "to score, or to scratch" and referring to designs scratched into plaster, revealing a different-colored surface underneath. This technique is also referred to as "crayon etching" or "crayon engraving."

Doing this project with two layers of crayons may be difficult for children under 5 years of age because a great deal of preparation is necessary. Given a small enough piece of paper to cover, however, even 4-year-olds can derive a great sense of accomplishment in what to them may seem like magic.

Materials
    Many colors of good-quality wax crayons
    Smooth pieces of cardboard, approximately 6" x 6" in size
    Round toothpicks

Procedure
Cover the cardboard solidly with the colored crayons. Cover the first layer of colors with a solid black crayon. Buff the top layer by rubbing it with a tissue or soft rag. Use the toothpicks to scratch a design through the top layer.

Variations
• Use a fingernail file instead of a toothpick.
• Use a carpenter's nail instead of a toothpick.
• Use solid dark blue, red, or some other dark color for the top layer.
• Use thick, creamy black tempera paint for the top layer. (Add a small amount of liquid soap to help the paint adhere to the waxy surface. Or dust the bottom layer with a bit of chalk from a blackboard eraser.)
• Use other colors of thick, creamy tempera for the top layer.
• Use diluted black India ink for the top layer.
• Use dark-colored crayons for the bottom layer and white tempera for the top to achieve a reversed effect.
• Vary the size and shape of the background cardboard.

Results
Making scratch boards may help children to
1. *increase their knowledge of linear design,*
2. *strengthen their powers of concentration, because of the extended nature of this project,*
3. *expand their consciousness of cause and effect,*
4. *understand that some activities require a sequence of steps, and*
5. *strengthen fingertip control as they make the scratching movements.*

GIANT SCRIBBLES

Materials
Large sheets of drawing paper, approximately 18" x 24"
An assortment of crayons

Procedure

Place paper and crayons on the floor. Encourage the children to cover their entire papers with scribbles.

Variations

• Use a much larger piece of paper, and have three or four children at a time work on the same piece.
• Divide an oversized circular piece of paper into four to six pieces, and have four to six children scribble at one time, each in his or her own section.

Results

This excellent developmental exercise may help children to
1. *strengthen their visual-motor coordination,*
2. *internalize the variety of shapes and lines that are the result of the scribbles, and*
3. *develop spatial awareness as they attempt to reach out and cover all areas of the large paper.*

ARM DANCING

Arm Dancing is my favorite developmental exercise. It is especially helpful for children who are not appropriately developing visual or auditory-perceptual skills.

Materials

A long roll of butcher, kraft, or brown wrapping paper, 30"–36", spread on the floor the length of the room

Three or four crayons for each child—dark colors are preferable

A record player and records with short musical selections, preferably without words (folk tunes, dance music, or classical pieces)

Procedure

Have each child lie down on the floor in front of one area of the

Arm Dancing, a group activity done to music. These children are all 3 years old. People of all ages perform this activity exactly the same way.

paper. There should be at least an elbow length between each child. Tell the children they can use the crayons to do "arm dancing." That is, they make big circles by moving the entire arm—they should not draw with wrist or finger movements, but rather make circles with shoulder and arm movements. Tell the children to listen to the music and try to move their arms in rhythm with the music. Tell them that every time the music stops, they can change to a new color of crayon. (The music should be stopped every 50 or 60 seconds and changed to another rhythm.)

It is important that *the circle be made directly in front of the child, so that the center of the circle lines up with the center of the body.* Developing children will often squirm slightly to one side or the other to avoid crossing the midline of the body.

Variations

- Children who are 5 years of age and older may make circles and then change to "lazy 8's"—that is, horizontal number eights, with the center of the 8 at the midline.
- Have children "dance" with both arms during one of the selections.
- Place large paper cutouts under the paper. As the children make their circles, the outlines will come into view.
- Have the children do arm dancing on individual sheets of 24" x 36" tagboard. They can use the same sheet several times.
- Conserve paper by using the arm dancing circles to paint over or by using the reverse side of the paper for painting.

Results

This valuable activity is an overall perceptual-motor development exercise for young children, as well as an excellent remediation for children in elementary grades who have even mild developmental lags. In doing this exercise, children

1. *relive the position of a 3-month-old infant who is just beginning to be able to cross the midline of the body,*
2. *coordinate their hearing, vision, and arm movements in one rhythmic pattern, internalizing that coordination for the development of their auditory-visual, auditory-motor, and visual-motor skills,*
3. *internalize the sensation of their arms moving rhythmically on a flat surface, which may later be evoked when they move their arms to do handwriting on a flat surface,*
4. *cross the midline of their bodies if they are helped to stay centered in front of their drawings (children who have not yet developed this skill find this very hard),*
5. *release pent-up feelings and ease tensions,*
6. *when using both arms, develop bilateral coordination,*
7. *when paper shapes are used, become aware of the constancy of shape, and*
8. *increase their overall sensory awareness.*

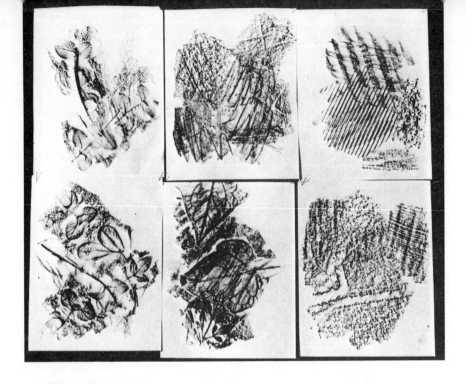

Crayon Rubbings made by rubbing the sides of crayons over objects with interesting textures.

CRAYON RUBBINGS

From infancy we depend greatly on our sense of touch to register minute details that our eyes fail to reveal about certain objects. And yet from an early age, children are told to keep their hands off things. The preschool teacher has the opportunity to *encourage* touching. Touching should be stimulated, talked about, and experienced. A good way to stimulate a child's sense of touch is to make rubbings.

Materials
A selection of peeled crayons
Typing, duplicator, or copy paper
Simple geometric shapes cut out of construction paper
Paper doilies

Procedure
Have the children arrange the doilies and cutouts under the

paper. Then have them rub the crayon over the paper, using the side of the crayon if they wish, until the outline of the shape shows through. Suggest to the children that they rub the crayon lightly so as not to tear the paper at the edges of the shapes.

Variations
- Use cutouts of animals or people.
- Use cutouts of flowers.
- Use cutouts of common objects.
- Vary the thickness of the cutouts.

(**Note:** The cutouts can be taken from old picture books that are no longer used for reading.)

Results
When doing crayon rubbings, children
1. *increase their knowledge of textures and shapes,*
2. *become more aware of cause and effect and of their ability to bring about changes,*
3. *learn that something does not have to be visible to the eye for a change to occur,*
4. *become aware of the delicate shading they can make with crayons,*
5. *sensitize their skills in tactile discrimination,*
6. *develop consciousness of the constancy of shapes and forms,*
7. *develop an understanding of the concepts of* over *and* under, *and*
8. *develop an understanding of the concepts of* thickness *and* flatness.

NATURE RUBBINGS

This activity uses the same materials and procedure as Crayon Rubbings, except that items from nature are used instead of cutouts.

Materials
> Leaves, grass, flower petals, clover, ferns, thin pieces of bark, weeds, and other growing things that the children help you select
>
> Drawing paper, butcher paper, brown wrapping paper, or similar paper in 9" x 12" or 12" x 18" sizes

Procedure
Have the children proceed as with the Crayon Rubbings, being careful to rub very lightly to avoid tearing the paper.

Variations
- Have the children make some designs with just leaves, some with just ferns, some with different kinds of weeds and grasses, and some with just bark.
- Have the children choose whatever pieces they want. Give them freedom to use whatever strikes their fancy in whatever arrangements they design.

Results
In addition to what children learn by doing rubbings (listed under Crayon Rubbings), they
> 1. *increase their awareness of the shapes found in nature, and*
> 2. *expand their awareness of the pleasures of creating designs from nature.*

STRING, YARN, AND OTHER WIGGLY THINGS

This continuation of the experiences with Crayon Rubbings requires much fingertip touching and shaping, enabling children to explore the textural qualities of the items. As they arrange their designs and bend and shape wires and pipe cleaners, the children use the small muscles of their hands and fingers. Each muscular movement is important to total development.

Materials

> String, yarn, ribbon, rubber bands, thin wires, pipe cleaners, and other wiggly or flexible things that children can manipulate with their hands to form shapes for rubbing

Procedure

The children arrange items to form designs. Then they place paper over the items and rub gently with crayons.

Children may want to assist one another in holding the paper firmly so that items won't shift around while being crayoned over.

Results

When children do rubbings of linear shapes, they not only gain the learnings from doing rubbings (listed under Crayon Rubbings, p. 87), but they may also

> 1. *increase their awareness of the possibilities of linear design shapes and*
> 2. *improve their motor coordination in two important ways: (a) by exercising the small muscles of the fingers and hands and (b) by practicing control of muscular pressure as they try to keep from tearing the paper while rubbing over it.*

OBJECT RUBBINGS

You can create additional rubbing experiences by having the children add rubbings of small, flat objects to previously created designs. Have the children help you collect paper clips, coins, metal washers, small pieces of screening, scraps of leather, Q-tips, and other small objects that are not so thick that they will cause the paper to tear too easily. Then they just put some of these objects under a paper with a rubbing already on it and do rubbings of them.

RUBBINGS WALK

Taking children on a rubbings walk is an intriguing activity and an excellent follow-up to any of the rubbings experiences.

Procedure

With crayon and paper, march around the room. Explore every nook. Try out every kind of surface. Look into drawers and under tables. Encourage the children to investigate all possibilities. Encourage them to find tempting surfaces to use for rubbings. They'll make many mistakes. Some items will make the paper tear, but that is something they should find out for themselves. Allow the children the freedom to experiment, and look for the creative ideas they come up with.

Results

In addition to the types of learning provided by rubbings activities, the Rubbings Walk gives children practice in
1. *making choices and decisions,*
2. *discriminating among alternatives, and*
3. *understanding the physical world.*

CRAYON RESIST

This project involves covering a crayon drawing or design with a liquid coating. The liquid, because it does not adhere to the wax, forms a colored background for the crayon markings. Children usually take special pride in their crayon resist pictures because of the magical effects and because of the beauty of even the simplest design done with this technique.

Materials

Good white drawing paper, butcher paper, tagboard, or any other paper that has a smooth, but not slick, surface (start out with 9" x 12" sheets and increase the size after the children have had experience with the technique)

Crayon Resist. Jenny and Matt (both 4½) are covering their papers with crayon. Then they will cover them with a thin wash of black tempera, which will enhance the brilliance of the colors. Scott (5) has already finished his.

Assorted colors of wax crayons

Thinned tempera or watercolor paint (start out with black or dark blue paint) and large brushes

Padding of several thicknesses of newspaper to provide a cushion to help make the crayon marks more intense

Procedure

Children make a scribble design or other type of drawing on the paper, pressing hard with the crayons to get a maximum amount of wax to adhere to the paper.

When the drawing is completed, the entire surface of the paper is washed over with a thin coating of paint.

Variations

• Use dark colors with light-colored paint.

• Substitute watercolor markers for the paint.

- Use only white crayons on white paper and any color of paint or ink. The white will faintly show up on the paper.
- Use white candles on white paper and any color of paint or ink. The wax will not show up at all until the paper is covered with ink or paint.
- Use black crayons on black paper with any color of paint to which white has been added to make the color more opaque.
- Instead of painting over the crayon marks, wet the entire paper. Shake off the excess water. Sprinkle drops of color on the paper, and spread it over the nonwaxed parts of the paper.
- Cover the drawing with a heavy coat of black tempera paint. When the paint has dried, hold the paper under running water so that most of the paint will wash off. Enough will probably adhere to the edges of the crayon marks to give the entire picture somewhat of a batik effect. (Care must be taken not to tear the paper when holding it under the water. One way to avoid tearing is to tape the paper on a flat board so that you can hold the paper under the water without sloshing it around.)

Results

Crayon resist activities enable children to
1. *observe that a surface covered with a waxy material will repel liquid,*
2. *further develop their muscles as they exert pressure with the crayons to obtain more brilliant colors,*
3. *increase their awareness of linear patterns and color contrasts, and*
4. *enhance their aesthetic appreciation, because of the lovely pictures they have created.*

BATIK

Materials

9" x 12" pieces of muslin, old sheeting, or other solid-color material

White crayons

Masking tape
Colored fabric-dye mixture

Procedure
Make scribbles or other designs on the fabric with the white crayons. Cover some parts with strips of masking tape. Dip the entire fabric into the dye. Wring it out, and hang it up to dry. When it is dry, remove the tape. The dye will have colored the fabric not covered by wax or tape.

Variations
• Use other colors of crayon than white.
• Use only various widths of masking tape. (Be sure that the tape is pressed down firmly along the edges.)
• Create batik designs on white T-shirts.

Results
The crayon batik project introduces the children to yet another way of using crayons. The experience forms a foundation for
1. *knowing that there are many ways of obtaining similar effects (the batik experience is similar to the crayon resist activities),*
2. *an increased awareness of patterns and designs on everyday fabric, and*
3. *a greater awareness of cause and effect.*

CRAYON ROLLS
Materials
Individual rolls of wide adding machine paper for each child
Assorted crayons for each child

Procedure
The rule is that paper must be unrolled from left to right. Sometimes I place the paper on the floor next to a wall in a position that allows it to be unrolled only to the right. You will

probably have to position the paper for the children before they use it.

Children may use crayons on the paper in whatever way they choose as long as they maintain the "unroll to the right" position.

Children's names can be placed on the edge of their own rolls. They can be allowed to choose to add to their rolls during any free activity period over a time span of several months.

Variations
- Obtain end rolls of paper from printing companies to use as depicted in the photo on page 65.
- Use long strips of paper that you have cut, and draw arrows pointing in the direction the children are to move toward.
- Use long strips of paper with yardsticks. Have the children use the edge of the yardstick to guide their crayon from left to right.
- Use pennant-shaped paper (see photos on p. 17 and p. 146) with a crayon container placed at the wide end of the paper, which should always be at the child's left because most children will draw on the large end first and move toward the pointed end. (If children don't do this, avoid telling them they are doing it wrong. Simply try another time or another type of project.) A good size for beginning pennant drawings is 12" at the wide end and 18" to 24" long. A true pennant shape is an isosceles triangle. In other words, the point is opposite the exact middle of the wide end.

Results
In doing Crayon Rolls, children prepare themselves for future writing experiences by
  1. practicing moving in left-to-right sequence and
  2. familiarizing themselves with utilizing different widths of space.

REPRESENTATIONAL DRAWINGS

Preschool children should not be made to feel that they *must* make a representational drawing at any time, nor should they be "taught" how to draw certain objects or figures. Step-by-step cartoon-type drawings of people, animals, and objects are very inappropriate for preschool children, although they may be greatly enjoyed by children of elementary school age. Even then, however, they should be used only as a "game" during play times, and not as part of an art program.

When children reach the age of 5 or 5½, they may begin to show an intense interest in representation. At that time, children should not be told, "Draw whatever you like." They respond best to guidance in the form of suggestions and motivation, such as the following:

- "If you could be an animal, draw what you would look like."
- "Next week we are going to visit the zoo. Draw a picture of an animal you might see there or of an imaginary animal that you make up in your own mind."
- "Here is a piece of round paper. Draw a picture inside the paper of how you think your face looks."
- "There are many children in our class. Draw a picture of one of the children. Or it can be yourself, someone in your family, or someone you just imagine. It does not have to be a real person."
- "Look at these pictures. See how many different kinds of trees there are. You can use your crayons to make up your own kind of tree."
- "We can use some beautiful flowers on our walls. What kinds of flowers can you design?"
- "Everyone seems (you seem) so sad today. Use the crayons to show me on the paper how sad (happy, excited, disappointed, hungry, etc.) you feel."
- "One time when I was on a trip, I saw lots of birds—big ones and little ones. Some were blue, some were black, some were gray, some were white, some were orange. They had all

different kinds of colors. Some had big wings and some had very little ones. Some had long legs and some had legs so tiny you could hardly see them. What kind of bird can you imagine?"
• "Pick something in the story to draw a picture about."
• "Draw a picture of your family."
• "Draw a picture of your house."

Caution: Avoid being judgmental. A person's creative efforts must be accepted on his or her own level. Some children have better perceptual images than others; some have better small motor coordination than others and can better produce those images. Avoid picking out the "best" pictures to display. If you display one, display all. Show appreciation for each child's drawing by mounting and displaying it with care.

Results
In doing representational drawings, children
   1. *display their developing ability to transfer mental images and memories of visual information onto paper, an important process in the development of cognitive skills,*
   2. *increase their ability to control fine motor movements, and*
   3. *experience making a plan and completing it, an important skill in the development of reasoning abilities.*

CHAPTER 5

Chalk and Other Drawing Materials

Soft, colorful, powdery chalk. Dry, talcumy, comfortable chalk. Like fine, dry dirt you may have played with on a hot summery day. It even clings to your hands like dirt, and if you touch something, the color comes off on what you touch. Magical chalk.

CHALK

The tactile effect of chalk, as it lightly and easily leaves its marks, is irresistible. Whether it is white chalk on a blackboard, large, colored lecturer's chalk, or bright-colored oil pastels on a big piece of scribble paper, chalk is irresistible.

TYPES OF CHALK

Because there are so many different types of chalk available today, you should make your selections carefully to get the greatest use of them.

Low-dust Chalk. If you have slate blackboards, try to obtain a low-dust brand of chalk. It usually comes in white or yellow (an easy-on-the-eyes color).

Chalkboard Chalk. If you have chalkboards instead of slate boards, it's best to purchase chalk made specifically for chalkboard use because it will be much easier to erase. This chalk is available in white, yellow (or yellow gold), and various colors.

Colored Drawing Chalk. A softer chalk is available for drawing on paper or other surfaces. Some brands are very soft and come off easily on the hands.

Oversized Chalk. These sticks of chalk are very easy for young children to grasp, as are oversized crayons.

Combination Chalk-Crayons. There are several brands of soft, waxy, crayonlike chalk that are interesting for occasional experimenting. They can be blended easily, and they are excellent for making scratch boards and crayon resist projects (see pp. 81–82 and 90–92). Check with your educational supply dealers for what is available. It is a good idea to buy just one box of any experimental material to try out before deciding to supply it for the children's occasional use.

Pastel Chalk. This is generally too soft for very young children to use satisfactorily. Kindergarten and elementary school children, if they have developed the skills to use art media with care, may want to experiment with some pastels.

Charcoal. Some charcoal, in addition to pastel chalk, should be available for occasional use by kindergarten and elementary school children. Charcoal is excellent to use when introducing these children to drawing still lifes or landscapes. You might be able to have an artist volunteer for some beginning instruction in these techniques.

CHALK EXPERIMENTS AND ACTIVITIES

DRY CHALK

Materials

Good drawing paper, white or light in color and with some
texture in order to grab the chalk
Selection of colored chalks

Procedure

Allow the children to color freely with the chalk, but remind
them not to press as hard as with crayons.

Variations

- Use light paper with dark colors of chalk.
- Use dark paper with light colors of chalk.
- Use colored chalk on a related color of paper. (Refer to "Color
  Wheel," p. 60.)
- Use highly textured papers, such as a good quality of watercolor paper, sandpaper, or any other paper with a rough
  finish, to achieve unusual effects.
- Use squares of Masonite as individual chalkboards. Try the
  back side for its rough texture. The smooth side can be
  sprayed with blackboard paint so that the chalk will adhere
  more readily.
- Use the chalk for "rubbings" activities in place of crayons, as
  described in Chapter 4, pages 86–90.

Results

*In using chalk on various papers and other surfaces, the
children will*

1. *develop a heightened awareness of color as they become
   aware of the many different shadings they can easily
   achieve,*

2. *improve their motor coordination as they learn to control the amount of pressure they use in applying the chalk,*
3. *increase their understanding of cause and effect as they learn that they can control the intensity and density of the colors by the amount of pressure they exert, and*
4. *develop new styles of linear design patterns to accommodate the lighter pressure needed to draw with chalk than with crayons.*

CHALK ON WET PAPER

Materials

An assortment of colored chalks

9" x 12" paper of a good quality for drawing on, and strong enough to withstand water

Several thicknesses of wet newspapers to place under the drawing paper to help keep its moisture during the activity

Procedure

Dip the paper in water before use, or sponge the surface of the paper with water.

Have the children apply the chalk to the wet paper in whatever manner they choose to do so.

Variation

• Vary choices of colors of paper and of chalk (as listed above under "Dry Chalk").

Results

When using chalk on wet paper, children will
1. *increase their sensitivity to color, because of the greater brilliance of chalk on wet paper than on dry paper,*
2. *become aware of new linear patterns, and*
3. *extend their knowledge of how materials change according to how they are used.*

Christine and Scott (both 5) experiment with chalk scribbles on paper covered with liquid starch.

MILK AND CHALK

Materials

Assorted colors of chalk

12" x 18" or larger sheets of good drawing paper

Procedure

Coat the paper with buttermilk. (Larger sheets can be used than when coating with water, because the buttermilk does not dry out as fast.)

Have the children apply the chalk to the paper.

Variation

• Use canned milk thinned with a little liquid starch instead of the buttermilk for a hard, waterproof finish.

Results

In using chalk on milk-dipped paper, the children will
1. *discover that the chalk will not rub off the finished picture, and*
2. *further increase their knowledge of change, as they realize the milk-dipped paper produces even more intensity in the colors than does water-dipped paper.*

FINGERPAINT CHALK

Materials

Assorted colors of chalk

Chalk drawings produced on milk-dipped paper as in the above activity

Containers of liquid starch or colorless fingerpaint

Procedure

Have the children fingerpaint over the chalked picture. Only the heavily chalked areas will color the fingerpaint media.

Variation

• Use white fingerpaint.

Results

When fingerpainting over previously chalked drawings, children will
1. *discover the process of fusion as some of the more heavily chalked areas provide a residue of color that mixes with the fingerpaint media, creating new patterns of color, and*
2. *internalize a knowledge of constancy as they discover that chalk, as a media, is less constant than crayon.*

WET CHALK

Instead of wetting the paper with water, buttermilk, or canned milk with liquid starch, the chalk itself can be dipped into the liquid.

Materials
>A small container of the liquid to be used or one large
>container for several children to share
>An assortment of chalks that have been soaking in the liquid
>for at least 5 minutes before use
>A choice of papers

Procedure
Encourage the children to explore the effect of the wet chalk on
the paper.

Variations
• Vary the colors of the chalk and the colors of the paper, using
  as a guide the suggestions made for varying the colors of
  crayons and paper in Chapter 4.
• Use seasonal colors similar to the suggestions in "Color Guide
  Through the Year" on pages 58–61.

Results
*When dipping the chalk into a liquid instead of wetting the
paper, the children will*
>1. *discover that an aim (in this case, brilliant chalk drawings)
>   can be achieved in more than one way, and*
>2. *discover that a process can be reversed and still achieve the
>   same results.*

SUGAR WATER AND CHALK
Instead of the liquids suggested in the previous activity, use
sugar water that has been mixed in a ratio of 1 cup of water to
$1/3$ cup of sugar. Be sure the sugar is well dissolved before use.

Procedure
Encourage the children to explore the effect of drawing with
chalk wet with sugar water.

Variation

• Use variations similar to those in previous chalk experiences about various color combinations of chalk and paper.

Results

When using the chalk dipped in sugar water, the children will
1. *observe the increased brilliance of the colors,*
2. *learn that the increased brilliance is caused by the reflection of the sugar crystals, even though they are not easily visible to the naked eye,*
3. *increase their awareness of cause and effect, and*
4. *add to their aesthetic appreciation as they respond to the beauty of the crystallized colors.*

CHARCOAL

Charcoal can be used for older children and adults. Although it is generally too delicate for preschool children, let them explore the use and capabilities of charcoal so that they will be familiar with it when they are older.

Materials

Small sheets of good drawing paper or charcoal paper
Small sticks of charcoal
Soft paper towels (kitchen type) or soft cloths

Procedure

Have the children explore the use of charcoal by finding out what kinds of lines they can make with it and how they can blend it by rubbing with a portion of a soft paper towel or cloth.

Variations

• Older children can use charcoal for still-life drawings.
• Older children can explore the shading of shapes by rubbing the charcoal gently into the space to be shaded.

• Older children can be given charcoal and charcoal paper for their first experiences in outdoor drawings of trees and landscapes.

Results
When using charcoal, children will
   1. *learn to hold the stick very delicately in order to keep it from breaking,*
   2. *learn to avoid exerting too much pressure to keep the point from breaking and to achieve the mark they want to make,*
   3. *become familiar with the wide variety of linear patterns they can make by gently applying the charcoal to the paper, and*
   4. *develop an awareness of the dramatic effect that can be achieved by the use of black and white.*

OIL PASTELS

These are similar to both chalk and crayons and may be used in the same ways as either. Pastels do not rub off as easily as chalk, however, and they are not quite as messy and are more easily controlled. Pastels are not as hard as crayons and break more easily, but they allow for much greater freedom of motion because they do not have to be pressed as hard as crayons to produce brilliant colors. Oil pastels come in many varieties. You should try one box of each of several brands before deciding which type you prefer to use with the children.

Materials
Good drawing paper that is not smooth
An assortment of oil pastels, or variations thereof
A soft rag with which to blend colors, if desired

Procedure
Encourage the children to explore the possibilities of the oil pastel on paper. Demonstrate how to blend the colors by rubbing them with a soft cloth.

Variations
- Combine the oil pastels with regular crayons.
- Older children may use a cloth that has had a small portion dipped into odorless thinner or odorless turpentine. Blotting the picture with such a cloth can create an oil-painting effect.

Results
When working with pastels, children will
>   1. *react to the fluidity and smoothness of the oil pastel as it glides across the surface of the paper and*
>   2. *find they are able to control the intensity of the colors by the amount of pressure they exert;*
>   3. *older children will grow in ego-strength and self-esteem as they realize their blotted pictures resemble oil paintings.*

FELT-TIP MARKERS

The transparency, brilliancy, and free flow of the color. The crystal brightness of their plastic containers. Their lightness and ease of use. All of these qualities make felt-tip markers a definite asset to any art program for young children and provide motivation and inspiration for their exploration and experimentation.

DRAWING WITH WATERCOLOR MARKERS

Watercolor markers are very appropriate for young children because they usually require only one stroke to get a definite mark—unlike other media. They are washable. They can be used on most absorbent surfaces, including papers and cardboards of all types, fabrics, styrofoam, soft, unpainted wood, and even unglazed pottery. They come in many varieties. It is a good idea to try single sets from different manufacturers until you find the ones that you prefer to use in your program.

107

Drawing with felt-tip markers. Varying stages of muscular control are evident in these drawings by Stephanie, Kerry, and Brian (all 3½) and Laura (4).

Since markers are costly, children should be taught the importance of always putting the lid back on a marker before picking up the next color. This practice can help your markers last a long time.

Materials

Assorted colors of markers

A choice of types and sizes of paper or other materials on which to draw

Protection for the table or other surface on which the markers will be used, because of their tendency to bleed through the paper

Procedure

Encourage the children to explore the use of the markers and to draw with them in the way they feel most comfortable.

Variations
- Use felt-tip markers for Arm Dancing (pp. 83–85).
- Use felt-tip markers for Crayon Resist in place of paint (pp. 90–92).
- Use felt-tip markers for Scratch Boards in place of the bottom layer of crayons (pp. 81–82).
- Use dark markers on light-colored paper.
- Use markers on a related color of paper (see "Color Wheel," p. 60).
- Use markers of a color that is complementary to the color of the paper (see "Color Wheel," p. 60).
- Use seasonal colors as suggested in "Color Guide Through the Year," pages 58–61.
- Combine markers with crayons and chalk.
- Wide-tip markers are best for preschool children, but fine-tip ones can be supplied from time to time for variety.

Results
When using watercolor markers, young children will
1. *increase their awareness of transparency, as they see the paper or other colors through the ink,*
2. *discover that because of the ink's transparency, markers do not show up well on dark papers,*
3. *expand their repertoire of linear design patterns because of the free flow of the markers' ink and the lack of a need to exert muscular pressure,*
4. *develop greater muscular control because of the lightness of the media, and*
5. *become aware of their responsibility in the care of the materials.*

PERMANENT MARKERS

Caution: Permanent markers are not a satisfactory medium for young children. The fumes can be injurious if inhaled.

Permanent markers should be reserved for people who are at least 10 years of age and who are able to use them carefully—not only because of the fumes, but also because they easily stain any surface with which they come in contact, and they readily bleed through paper and cloth.

For older children and adults, permanent markers are an excellent medium for marking on nonporous surfaces such as glass, metal, ceramics, or painted wood, or for permanent marks on fabrics. They are also excellent for use on items exposed to the weather and for creating signs and posters.

NOVELTY CRAYONS AND MARKERS

There are many novelty crayons, chalks, and markers now being marketed commercially. These are fun to experiment with, but caution should be taken in substituting novelty markers—that may not always be available and that are sold primarily as gimmicks—for traditional, readily available markers. The primary question to ask when considering novelty markers is whether they will provide valuable new learning experiences.

OTHER DRAWING MEDIA

GLASS WAX DRAWINGS

Materials
Glass wax (nontoxic)
A cloth
A window
Plenty of clean rags or paper towels (for cleanup)

Procedure
Children use the cloth to apply the wax to the surface of a

window. Allow it to dry for a few minutes. They then use their fingers to make linear designs and other marks on the window through the wax.

Variations
- Use a thin paste of mud instead of the glass wax.
- Use a paste of water and Bon Ami in place of the glass wax. Experiment with adding small amounts of powdered tempera to the mixture.

Results
When drawing with glass wax, children will
  1. *be surprised by the ease with which they can make clear marks on the window with a very light touch of the hand,*
  2. *extend their sensory and tactile awareness as they experience the sensation of drawing through the wax, and*
  3. *realize the finality of their movements, for, unlike crayons or chalks, once the wax creating the mark is removed, they can't change their marks.*

DRAWING IN MUD OR WET SAND

Universally, children like to draw pictures and designs in mud and wet sand. Search out such areas and introduce your children to this natural media.

Materials
  Twigs or other "found" natural material with which to make the drawings
  Plenty of paper towels, buckets of soapy water, perhaps a hose, and other materials needed to clean up afterward

Procedure
Encourage children to explore the possibilities of nature's drawing board.

A bowl of mud and a little encouragement from the teacher started Kristen, John, and Leo (all 5) on a unique drawing experience that provided much kinesthetic satisfaction. Afterward, the teacher and children together cleaned up the mess with a hose and paper towels.

Results

When drawing in mud or wet sand, children will
1. *experience emotional satisfaction as they realize that "playing in the mud" is an acceptable activity and*
2. *gain new eye-hand coordination skill when they use long twigs for this activity.*

DRAWING WITH PENCILS

Materials

A kindergarten-sized pencil for each child
Drawing paper

Procedure

Encourage children to use the pencil on paper for whatever types of markings or scribbles they wish to make.

Variation

• Occasionally supply some good-quality colored pencils. Pencils that are not of good quality have a very poor color, are hard to use, and are not satisfying to the user.

Results

When children are allowed to scribble freely with pencils, they will

1. *expand their knowledge of linear design in black and white without the added stimuli of color and*
2. *become more aware that many different media can be used to achieve similar results.*

Painting with Brushes

*"Drip. Drip. Drip. Yelllllllllllooooooooooow. Yel—llllll—
ooowwwwwww. Drip it. Drip it. Drip it." Here was music
coming from 3½-year-old Lynne, who was immersed in her
own private world of color. I had been teaching for several
years. I was developing ideas on creative teaching, but I
didn't yet understand. For I intruded on that little girl's
world and said, "What a beautiful song. We'll all help you
sing it." I cleverly gathered several children around me and
asked them to join with me in singing, "Drip. Drip. Drip.
Yelllllllllllooooooooooow. Yel—llllll—ooowwwwwww. Drip
it. Drip it. Drip it." Some of the children joined in. But my
little friend, my creator of songs, did not. With a disinter-
ested shrug, she put down her paintbrush, left her paper, and
walked away. Soon she was sitting in the boat, seeking solace
from the soothing effect of its rhythm as it rocked to and fro.*

BASIS FOR COMMUNICATION

The painting experience enables children to wander into far-
away, undiscovered lands. As they confront the painting surface with color-saturated brushes or other implements, their
imaginations begin to soar. As they begin to apply the paint,
and as their emotions begin to interact with the medium, the

outside world and the people around them fade into a remote distance. The painting, the color, and the self become one. Whether the spell is momentary or whether it lasts for several minutes, the experience refreshes the spirit and the mind, providing a basis for communication that is not dependent on verbalization.

TEMPERA PAINT

Painting is such an important influence on the overall growth of developing children that much care should be taken in the selection and presentation of the painting materials. Tempera paint is probably the most satisfactory type of paint for general use by children. It is a very easy medium to control. Since tempera paint is water soluble, its density can be varied by the amount of water or other liquid added to it. Tempera paint dries quickly, and, once dried, it can be painted over. It combines well with other media, allowing for much diversity of use. In addition, using tempera paint enables children to develop skills that they can apply to many other types of art media as well as to the performance of future academic tasks.

PURCHASING TEMPERA PAINTS

In purchasing tempera paints, it is advisable to stick to well-known brands. Inexpensive or substandard brands may result in washed-out, weak colors. In selecting the paint you want to use with children, consider the following questions:

1. Are the paints nontoxic?
2. Are the colors bright and clear?
3. Do the colors mix well together?

4. Are they washable? (Some colors will stain in almost any brand, but some brands are more stain-resistant than others.)
5. Is the texture of the liquid tempera creamy?
6. Does the liquid tempera come in nonbreakable containers?
7. Does the liquid tempera pour easily?

Washable Liquid Tempera
There are now on the market totally washable paints. The colors are not quite as pronounced as those in the standard tempera, but these washable paints are certainly recommended for use with very young children, especially those under 4 years of age. The brightness and intensity of the totally washable and nonstaining colors will probably improve as the demand for them grows.

COLORS OF TEMPERA

Start out with the three primary colors (see "Color Wheel," p. 60): *red, blue,* and *yellow.*

Add two secondary colors: *green* and *orange.*

Then add *brown, black,* and *white.*

These will give you sufficient colors for a fulfilling art program.

When you feel you can handle it, cautiously add *purple* (including violet, magenta, red violet, and related colors). These colors stain easily, so their use needs to be controlled a little more than that of the other colors.

If your budget allows, supplement your basic supply with additional colors, such as *dark green, turquoise blue, yellow green, blue green, red orange, yellow orange, peach,* and *bright red.* Although many of these colors can be mixed by combining primary and secondary colors, the tempera mixtures will not always have the same brilliance and clarity as the commercially prepared paints. With or without these added colors, however, color mixing should be a part of your agenda.

COLOR MIXING

During the fall and winter months of the school year, use your paints as they are. Later on, as spring approaches, you can begin to mix many of your own colors to use with the pure colors. Don't be afraid to experiment. Follow these guidelines to produce new colors:

1. Begin by adding a very small quantity of one color of paint to another.
2. Increase the amount as needed.
3. Always start out with the lighter color and gradually add the darker color.
4. Mix or stir the colors gently to avoid oxidation, which causes a loss of intensity.
5. When mixing powdered paints, mix the dry powders before adding the liquid. Experiment with very small quantities to get the proportion of each color that will achieve the desired effect.

Tints. Mix tints by adding the desired base color to a little white. Add more white as needed to achieve the desired tint.

When a color is mixed with white, that color becomes opaque. The more white added, the greater the opaqueness.

Shades. Adding a very small amount of black to a color will shade that color. An eyedropper is a convenient tool for adding black a few drops at a time.

Grayed Colors. These muted colors are achieved by adding a very small quantity of the opposite color to the paint. (See "Color Wheel," p. 60, for how to determine true opposites.)

ADDITIONAL TIPS FOR COLOR MIXING

Browns. Red, blue, and yellow make brown. Mix them in equal parts, and then add more of any one of the three colors as needed to get the particular shade of brown you desire.

Any two complementary colors will also make brown. Thus, green (which is a combination of blue and yellow) and red make brown. Violet (which is a combination of red and blue) and yellow make brown. Other combinations you can use are orange and blue, red orange and turquoise, and magenta and yellow green.

A penetrating deep brown can be created by adding red to black. You may need to add a small amount of green or yellow to get the desired shade.

Greens. For blue green, start with blue and add just enough yellow to give the greenish tinge you are seeking.

For yellow green, start with yellow (even though it is the lighter color) and gradually add small quantities of blue, a little at a time, until the desired shade is reached.

For chartreuse, add small amounts of black to yellow.

Dark green can be made by adding as much black as is needed to get the desired color. You might want to experiment with adding minute quantities of either red or purple, or both, to get a deeper green.

Reds. A deep carmine can be obtained by adding traces of blue to red.

Red orange is obtained by adding a small quantity of red to orange.

For an unusual grayed effect, add traces of black and yellow to red. Add white to vary the value. Or try it without the yellow.

Cerise can be obtained by adding orange and magenta to a very small quantity of red.

Blues. Blues can be varied greatly by adding traces of yellow or green.

Small amounts of magenta added to blue will increase its intensity without changing the color.

Blue mixed with small amounts of black and orange will give an interesting grayed effect, which can be further varied by the addition of white.

Yellows. Vary yellow slightly by adding traces of orange and a trace of white.

Or add a very small trace of black with a little white.

Gray the yellow with a minute amount of violet.

Oranges. Magenta added to orange produces a luminous red orange, which can be varied by the addition of small amounts of either white or yellow, or both.

Orange can also be varied by adding either yellow or red, or both.

Orange can be grayed by adding traces of blue. Vary it further by adding traces of black or white, or both.

Violets. Violet can be varied by the addition of magenta, blue, or red.

Add blue and white to violet to obtain luminous lavender.

Adding traces of green and black will give a gray effect, which can be further varied by adding white.

Black. If you have no black paint, mix red, blue, and green (or red, blue, and yellow—depending on the brand of paint) for a substitute.

CONTAINERS

When selecting paint containers, you should consider both aesthetic and practical qualities. Glass containers, although attractive, are not practical because of the danger of breakage. Clear plastic containers that let the color show through are as attractive as glass ones yet are safer to use. Colored plastic containers, with lids, are available from educational supply companies.

Food cans make ideal paint containers for 2- to 4-year-olds. The 6-ounce cans that tomato paste comes in are excellent for little fingers to wrap around. You can use 12-ounce cans for children 4 years old and over.

Prepare cans for use as paint containers with the following steps:

1. Apply a white undercoat over the outside of the can.
2. Paint over the undercoat with bright glossy enamel. Use one of your commonly used tempera colors for each can. You may be able to obtain the colors you need from a hobby shop, since you will only use a small amount of each one.

   Instead of buying enamels, you may paint the cans with the appropriate colors of tempera. To make the tempera waterproof, mix the paint with an equal amount of canned milk. When the paint is dry, spray it with several coats of plastic, or cover it with a clear shellac.
3. Prepare several cans in black or white for storing new color mixtures, seasonal colors, and others that don't match the prepared cans.

BRUSHES

EASEL BRUSHES

Easel brushes are commonly used for tempera painting. Provide a variety of sizes and styles. Generally, long-handled brushes allow for the greatest freedom of movement. They are most highly recommended, except for the youngest children. (See "Other Brushes" below.)

Quality is important when purchasing brushes. Better brushes are set in seamless aluminum or nickel-plated ferrules (holders), which are rustproof. They hold the bristles well, and the handles won't come loose. Bristle (hog hair) brushes are most commonly used. Be sure to obtain brushes with long bristles, which have greater flexibility.

Brush ends that are flat and long are called flats. Those that are rounded and tapered are called rounds. Both types should be provided in fairly large sizes ($^3/4$" to $1^1/4$").

OTHER BRUSHES

In addition to the traditional bristle brushes, provide the children with some brushes with softer bristles.

Short, stubby, fat brushes with nylon hairs are easy for 2- and 3-year-olds to use. They are very long lasting.

Camel hair is the name commonly applied to brushes made of squirrel hair. Or they are sometimes made from pony or cattle hair. Some camel hair brushes are very cheaply made.

Ox hair brushes are good for working with thick paint, such as paint mixed with milk to get a waterproof finish.

Sable brushes are expensive and are not necessary for young children. However, it is helpful to have a few sable brushes on

hand for elementary school art projects that may require precision painting.

Nylon brushes with long handles and small tips should be reserved for projects that use acrylic paints, since they are easier to clean and care for with this fast-drying media.

Bristle-haired varnish brushes (1½" to 2" or 3") are good for covering large surfaces.

CARE OF TOOLS

Whether you are using some twigs found out in the yard or the most expensive sable paintbrushes, your painting tools should be handled with care. How you handle materials provides a model for children and gives them a message about how important you think creative activities are.

Help to instill in the children a respect for the creative

process. The gentleness and pride with which you handle these tools will help them develop an appreciation of the wonders that can come from a few simple art materials.

PAINTING SURFACES

You don't have to use expensive easels to paint on. You can use table tops, floors, walls, or any other surface that is easy for children to reach. Given a choice, in fact, most very young children's first choice would be to paint on the floor, and their second choice would be to stand at a table to paint.

Large pieces of Celotex make good painting surfaces for Marty and Susan (both 5).

WHY TABLE-TOP PAINTING?

I encourage table-top painting for preschool children because it is comfortable for them. When paint is placed to their left, the children get practice in moving their eyes from left to right, the direction they will use in reading and writing. Table-top painting also minimizes the problem of dripping paint that accompanies easel painting. The ideal approach is, however, to provide a wide variety of surfaces and angles at which to paint, thus providing the children with opportunities to develop a wide variety of eye-hand coordination patterns.

☐ **Note:** I suggest that you copy the above paragraph and insert it in your parent handbook to offset any disappointment when parents do not see "cute" easels in the classroom.

TABLE-TOP PREPARATION

Be sure the tables are low enough so that the children can move their arms freely and in natural positions while they are painting.

Cover the table with a protective covering such as plastic or oilcloth. I buy clear plastic, #4–#6 weight, because it is easy to handle. It's heavy enough to stay in place, easy to wipe clean, and light enough to fold easily for storage.

Newspapers also make excellent coverings because they can be discarded after use. Some persons have an allergy to newsprint ink, however, so take this into consideration. To avoid the problem, you can use unprinted newspaper stock, which is available at little or no cost from newspaper companies or at very low cost from paper supply companies. Wrapping paper can also be used and discarded after several uses, and you do not have to worry about ink sensitivity.

Whatever covering you use, make the children comfortable

by arranging the covering, materials, and equipment in such a way that they will not have to worry about making a mess.

CELOTEX PAINTING BOARDS

Celotex, a material generally obtainable from lumber yards, has the advantage of versatility. Celotex resembles plasterboard but has a soft finish on both sides. It makes an excellent surface for bulletin boards.

Celotex comes in 4' x 8' sheets. They can be sawed easily into two equal halves (4' x 4'), which makes a good size for placing on top of the average table in a preschool. If you use 5' or 6' tables, you can cut the Celotex accordingly.

Ways to Use Celotex Painting Boards

1. Place the Celotex squares on top of the tables. Because the children stand at each side of the board to paint, two to four children can work comfortably at the same time, depending on the size of the paper.
2. Place the Celotex on the floor, with a 2" x 4" block of wood under each corner so that the children can get down on their knees to paint. This method is especially good for making very large paintings that encourage children to reach and stretch as they apply the paint to the farthest reaches of the paper.
3. Occasionally, use 4" or 6" supports for the board. Each height provides a slightly different eye-hand coordination exercise.
4. Stand the boards against the wall, using them like easels. Paper is easily fastened to the boards with pushpins.
5. Place the paint on a chair, a stool, or even a cardboard grocery carton or a crate standing on end next to the wallboard or in front of it, as shown in the photo on page 135.

6. Take the Celotex boards outdoors and stand them against a fence or a wall. Place the paints on a playground bench, a box, a stool, or a chair.

If Celotex is unavailable in your community, substitute sheets of corrugated cardboard. You can purchase large sheets from a paper supply company or cut out the sides of a cardboard refrigerator, washing machine, or other large appliance container.

STANDARD EASELS

Standard children's easels are nice to have, even though they are not a necessity. If you do use them, be sure that you give the children *equal time* to paint on horizontal surfaces, such as table tops or boards on the floor, as previously described. Different visual perception and eye-hand coordination skills are exercised by each method.

If standard easels are used, they should be kept clean of paint. Just as with other art materials, easels should always be neat and presented in a caring manner, rather than allowed to accumulate paint spills and streaks month after month.

CARDBOARD EASELS

Convenient table-top easels can be made out of cardboard, as shown in the diagram on page 129.

Materials
2 sheets of cardboard, 18" x 24" or larger (so that you can use 18" x 24" pieces of paper)

Duct tape or other cloth tape
2 yards of heavy yarn or cotton cord

Procedure

Fasten a strip of tape along the top and bottom edges of the two pieces of cardboard as a protective measure.

Cut 6" strips of tape with which to hinge the two pieces of cardboard together.

Stand the two pieces in an upside-down V shape, adjusting them to a sturdy balance, and then tape them together at the top.

To keep the angle at an appropriate width, you can punch a hole near the bottom of each side of the two pieces of cardboard and run the cord or yarn through those holes. Tie the cord or yarn to maintain the angle.

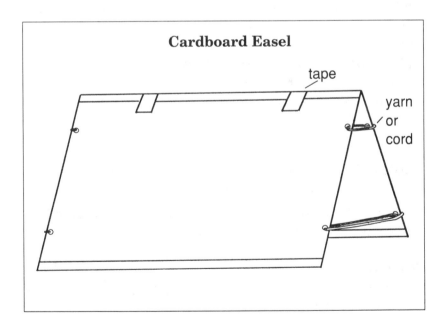

Cardboard Easel

tape

yarn or cord

CONDUCTING THE ACTIVITY

When the children are going to paint, you can make them and yourself more at ease by anticipating the possibility of spilled or splattered paint. Provide aprons for teachers and children and protective coverings for table tops, floors, and any other surfaces that might not be easy to clean.

HAND WASHING

If you have a sink in the classroom, that is fine for hand washing. But if there is no water immediately available, place a pail of warm soapy water next to the paint area for rinsing paint off the hands before regular washing later. Have paper towels available for drying hands, and sponges for cleanups.

SOME GUIDELINES FOR PAINTING

Provide paper, paint, brushes, and any other materials necessary for the activity you have planned.

1. Encourage the children to keep the paints to the left side of the paper, whether they are painting at an easel, on a table top, or on the floor. *This helps children internalize a left-to-right orientation* that will be important for reading and writing.
2. When several children are painting around a table, set the paints in the center and have the children take the color they want to use and place it to their left, in order to encourage left-to-right movement.
3. Usually, no directions should be given to the children except those that may be needed to help them understand and

Teri (2) grips her paintbrush in a way that will require her to make bold arm movements. Stevie (3½) is able to use a gentler, more mature grip that allows him greater control of the brush.

control both the materials and their emotions. The care with which you plan and set out the materials should motivate most of the children to use them in specific ways.

☐ **Note:** When a child uses the materials you have set out for a specific project in a different way than you had expected, look upon it as a creative act. Learning does not occur from one activity alone, but rather from the culmination of all activities and experiences. It is a mistake to assume that we always know what a child is learning at any particular time; the lesson may not be the one we had anticipated. The important goals are the involvement, the movement, and the discovery of self-accomplishment. In other words, *the process, not the product*, is important to child development.

4. Give the children as much freedom of time, space, and use of the materials as your facilities and supervisory help will allow.
5. As often as possible, allow children to paint more than one picture if they want to.

NAMES

Children's names should consistently be placed in the upper left corner of their paintings. This will get the children accustomed to looking in that corner, which will be important when they begin to learn to read and write, because they will have already acquired the habit of starting in the upper left-hand corner.

PAINTING EXPERIENCES WITH COLOR

Additional awareness of the possibilities of color and paint can be attained through the variation of the ways in which the materials are presented.

There are many ways to paint with tempera to provide different kinds of learning experiences for the young child. Here are some suggestions.

FREE PAINTING

The suggestions given under this heading, "Free Painting," should be applied to all of the painting experiences that follow. Many of the suggestions will lend themselves to the use of other types of art media as well.

Colors

In all painting experiences, provide a selection of colors, varying them from day to day or week to week. Follow the guidelines in "Color Guide Through the Year," pages 58–61, as well as some of the suggestions at the beginning of this chapter for varying individual colors.

The 2-year-old should be given only two or three colors to use at any one time.

The 3-year-old should be given from two to three colors most of the time, gradually building up to four or five colors after much experience.

The 4- and 5-year-olds should be given a variation in the number of colors. Sometimes they should be given only two, sometimes three, sometimes four or five, and sometimes six or more.

The experienced, talented, or older child can be allowed to select from six to eight colors, learning to use the color wheel to plan combinations that are naturally harmonious, contrasting, or psychedelic.

Brushes

Good brushes should always be provided, unless an alternative type of painting tool is being explored. Allow the children to use the brushes in their own way, as long as they don't mistreat them. Remind the children to keep each brush in the color of paint it starts out in. Teach the children to participate in cleaning the brushes when the paints are put away for the day.

Results

Free painting—the free exploration of colors and the free use of individual brush techniques—helps children to

1. *set their own standards and realize their own capabilities,*
2. *discriminate in choice of materials and in methods of application,*
3. *exercise the large arm muscles and fine motor muscles,*

4. *develop eye-hand coordination and visual perceptual skills,*
5. *internalize concepts of arrangement and shapes of spatial forms,*
6. *gain an aesthetic appreciation of design and color balance,*
7. *try out ideas, test their skills, and refine their techniques, and*
8. *express their feelings and release their emotions in a sound and healthy, and sometimes therapeutic, manner.*

DRIP PICTURES

This is an excellent rainy-day project because you can fasten the paper to a window wall, if you have one, and let the rain provide the background.

Materials

Easels or paint boards that are placed upright against a wall

Rectangular paper, mounted vertically

Paint that is mixed slightly thinner than usual but is not watery (it should drip rather slowly down the paper)

3 to 5 colors of paint plus white (for 2-year-olds, use three colors, and add white for those who are more experienced and can handle the fourth color without confusion)

Brushes—the fullest-bodied ones you have

Butcher paper, plastic, or other material to protect the surface underneath the paper and easels where the paint will drip

Procedure

Demonstrate to the children how a full brush of paint can be pressed firmly against the paper to squeeze out the paint, which will then drip down the paper. This will evolve into a self-teaching experience when the children discover that if a full brush allows the paint to drip, then wiping the brush on the

Drip Pictures. By learning how to make the paint drip down a vertical surface, Ken and Karen (both 3) will be able to figure out for themselves how to prevent paint from dripping when they do other kinds of painting.

edge of the container so that it has less paint on it will prevent dripping.

Variations
- Use very long, narrow paper.
- Drip paint directly on tall cardboard boxes.
- Use pastel colors against a dark background.
- Use only related colors, plus white.
- Use a psychedelic combination, plus white.
- Use only primary colors.
- Use only secondary colors.
- Create a mural with several children working on the painting at the same time.

Results
This self-teaching experience with dripping paint helps children to
1. *experiment to get a desired effect,*
2. *become more aware of cause and effect,*
3. *develop temporal concepts because some colors drip faster than others, depending on the density of the paint, and*
4. *begin to learn the concept of representational painting when the drip paintings are done on a rainy day and the children relate their dripping colors to the rain. (Note: Not all 2- and 3-year-olds can make this connection, but most children can by the time they are 4.)*

DROP PAINTINGS

Doing *Drip Pictures* leads to an interest in doing *Drop Paintings*. This is a good project to do outdoors, especially on a grassy area, although the pictures may be done indoors too. (See also *Splatter Paintings* below.)

Materials
36"- wide (or wider) wrapping or butcher paper placed flat on the floor (see photo on p. 137)
Plastic, paint boards, newspaper, or other materials to protect the surface underneath and around the edges of the painting
Paint that is slightly thinned out, but not watery
Many colors of paint
The largest and fullest easel brushes you have

Procedure
The children stand at the edge of the paper, each holding a container of paint. Demonstrate how to dip the brush in the container, pull it out without wiping it on the edge of the container, and hold it over the paper, with arm outstretched.
The paint is allowed to drop and splash as it will. The

Drop Painting. Anne, Terry, and Terri (all 5) have developed sufficient control of their finger movements to direct the paint where they want it to drop without flicking their wrists and making it splash.

children can move around the edge of the paper to allow the paint to drop in different area.

Rule: When performing this activity indoors, shaking the brush is not allowed. Outdoors, it is OK.

Variations
- Several children can work on the painting at one time, with shifts rotating to work on the same painting.
- After the painting is dry, have several children drop some white and some black in a few areas of the painting. These form a defined contrast to some of the colors that may have run together.
- Use all pastel colors.
- Use only related colors.
- Use only primary and secondary colors.

Results

Drop painting can help children to

1. become aware of the color patterns that can be formed by dropping and splashing colors in a controlled area as they change colors and move around the paper to create new patterns,
2. learn how to control the amount of paint on the brush after discovering that more paint will drop from a full brush,
3. develop muscular control as they hold the brush over the paper, waiting for the paint to drop off of it,
4. develop wrist control as they learn to wiggle the wrist very slightly—in fact, almost imperceptibly—to encourage the paint to drop, yet at the same time not to shake the wrist so hard that the paint will splatter all over,
5. develop patience as a result of having to wait for the paint to drop,
6. develop temporal awareness, also as a result of having to wait,
7. participate in group planning as the surface becomes covered and thought has to be given to where additional paint needs to be added and what color it should be, and
8. increase their awareness of spatial relationships between themselves and other children as they take care not to splash paint on their own or others' shoes or clothing.

SPLATTER PAINTINGS

This activity is the same as *Drop Paintings*, except that it is always done outdoors, where the paint can be splattered and splashed more freely.

For this project, it is best for children to work individually or in groups of two or three.

Materials

Smaller pieces of paper than for the *Drop Paintings*
Paint prepared as for *Drop Paintings*

Protection for the background surface
Aprons
A hose with which to wash away the paint from the ground
after the project is completed

Procedure
Proceed as in *Drop Paintings,* except that children may splatter
and splash more freely, but they still must take care not to get
paint on themselves or others.

Variations
• First splatter light colors over the background. Then splatter
dark colors on top of the light ones.
• Reverse the above procedure, using dark colors first and then
light colors.
• Use black paper with bright colors splattered over it.

Splatter Painting. Kari, Julie, and Laura (all 4) learn to control their wrist
movements to splatter their paints on various parts of the paper.

- We frequently use our discarded Celotex paint boards for this project. By splattering bright, fresh colors over the boards and then adding some splashes of white for the finishing touch, we create lovely abstract paintings. We have frequently traded these paintings to parents for outgrown tricycles and other toys. The parents frame the paintings and hang them in their homes. One pediatrician hung such a painting, 8' x 4', in his office. He said that most of the children who came to see him called the painting "Stars."
- Adding milk to the paints for this project makes it more permanent.

Results
This expressive splash-and-splatter experience enables children to

1. *extend the learnings gained from their previous experiences of making Drip Pictures and Drop Paintings,*
2. *expand their awareness of color and color mixtures as the paint intermingles on the paint surface,*
3. *intensify their awareness of surrounding spaces as they shake the brush in an attempt to get the paint on the* paper only *and not on the surrounding surface,*
4. *increase their awareness of the needs of others as they take care not to get paint on those standing or working nearby, and*
5. *develop responsibility as they assist in cleaning up the really big mess this project makes.*

WET COLOR
Materials
Paper that has been wet thoroughly before use (blot puddles with a sponge)
Paint mixed to a medium consistency, in colors that will blend fairly well together
A brush for each color of paint

Procedure
Children drop the paint onto the paper or apply it directly with the brush, allowing the colors to run together.

Variations
• Use watercolor instead of tempera.
• Use eyedroppers and food coloring mixed with water instead of brushes and paint.

Results
These experiments help children to
  1. *develop an understanding of the design possibilities in the simple interaction of paint and water,*
  2. *appreciate the element of surprise as the paint and water mix in unexpected ways, and*
  3. *know that they cannot always control the media they use in the way that they want to.*

WRINKLED COLOR

Materials
  Paper that has been thoroughly crushed and then dipped in water and straightened out
  Paints and brushes or eyedroppers and food coloring (as in the above activity)

Procedure
Proceed as for *Wet Color,* noting that the colors will be emphasized in the lines formed by the wrinkles.

Results
This project helps children to
  1. *understand the meaning of* wrinkled, *and thus of its opposite,* smooth, *and*
  2. *know that they cannot always control media the way they want to.*

DRY COLOR

Reverse either of the above two experiences by using dry paint with very wet brushes and either wet or dry paper.

Materials

Dry paper and wet paper

Large brushes

Container of water in which to wash the brushes in between each use

Paper towels to help wipe the paint out of the brushes

Powdered paint in small containers

Procedure

Note: Put out very small amounts of powdered paint at a time—about 2 tablespoons. By keeping the amounts small and always handling the powder gently, you minimize the potential for the children to inhale any of its dust. Always shake powdered paint onto paper with small, table-sized salt shakers; do not use the large cooking size. The smaller the shaker, the less the potential for paint dust in the air.

Dip the brush in water. Then dip the wet brush in the powdered tempera.

Apply the brush to the dry paper experimentally.

Repeat the procedure with several colors, rinsing out the brush thoroughly between colors.

Variations

• Use wet paper instead of dry.

• Use a slightly damp brush instead of a wet one, thus picking up less paint, and apply the paint to wet paper.

• Use cotton balls to pick up the powder.

• Pick up paint with a wad of folded facial tissue that has been partially dipped into water.

• Gently sprinkle powdered tempera from a small salt shaker onto wet paper.

Results

Applying dry tempera to paper helps children to

1. *increase their knowledge of differences between things that are wet and things that are dry,*
2. *heighten their appreciation of the visual impact of pure color, and*
3. *internalize the concept of reversal of processes, thus encouraging the imaginative use of materials and techniques.*

PAINTING EXPERIENCES WITH SHAPES

OVERSIZED PAINTINGS

Having children make oversized paintings is an excellent perceptual motor development project because of the reaching and stretching involved. This project is usually done on the floor.

Materials

Oversized sheets of paper on which to paint, preferably 3' x 5' if you have 36"-wide paper available, or you can cut circular shapes 36" in diameter or paste two pieces of 36"-wide paper together to make an even bigger circle

Protection for the surface surrounding the paper

Selected paints in containers

Brushes in the paint containers

Procedure

The oversized paper is placed so that one edge is against a wall. This requires the children to reach and stretch as they cover all areas of the paper.

The paint and brushes are placed to the left of the paper. The children are allowed to proceed without any specific directions. Some will kneel, some will sit (see photo on p. 125), and some will even stoop while painting.

The circular shape of the oversized sheet of paper inspires the relaxed actions by Bret (5) as he explores the space involved. Compare Bret's posture with that of the two children in the picture on page 125.

They usually react according to the size and shape of the painting surface. Circular paper, for example, seems to inspire a very gentle, relaxed pose (see photo above). Rectangular paper, with its sharp corners, seems to be more conducive to rigorous action. As the children attempt to cover the various parts of the paper with paint, they must decide whether to move to another side of the paper or whether to reach across the paper.

Variation
• A large paper can be placed on the floor in the center of the room. Divide the paper into four areas: top right, top left, bottom right, and bottom left. One child is assigned to each area to paint a picture. Sociability and cooperation are the goals in this variation, as opposed to the perceptual motor goals of the primary activity.

Results

In painting oversized pictures, children learn to
  1. *understand shape (the shape of the paper) in relation to their own movements,*
  2. *enhance problem-solving skills and increase their ability to make decisions as they decide how to move to paint the paper,*
  3. *develop eye-hand coordination as they move from the paint container to the far reaches of the paper (a different position than they are accustomed to),*
  4. *evaluate spatial relationships and internalize specific experiences that can later be transferred to other undertakings in life, such as plotting a garden, planning a mural, setting up a bulletin board, planning furnishings for a room, or laying out a diagram for an outdoor game or game court, and*
  5. *take pride in accomplishing such a large painting, which is so very noticeable, and thus increase their self-esteem.*

PENNANTS, WANDS, AND PAPER ROLLS

Painting on pennant shapes is another visual-motor perceptual exercise that trains children to work from left to right, a skill they will need when they learn to read and write. This activity is based on the fact that most children (and adults, too) will start painting on the wide part of the paper, moving toward the pointed end as the work progresses.

Materials

  Pennant-shaped pieces of paper, cut as isosceles triangles (the diagrams on p.147 show how to cut the paper for the proper shape and the greatest economy)

  Various sizes of the paper (the larger they are, the more unique the experience)

  Two, three, or four paint colors at the most

Flag Making. Chris and Keith (both 5) are handling their brushes in a mature way as they allow the pennant-shaped paper to influence their movements from left to right.

Procedure

The paper should be set down before the child with the wide end to the child's left, and the paint containers and brushes should be placed by the wide end of the paper. **Note:** If the child turns the paper around and ends up with the position reversed or moves the paint and brushes to the opposite side, don't worry. The left-to-right progression may take place anyway. If not, it will be learned through other experiences. The *autonomy* demonstrated by the child in changing the position of the paper is an equally important learning experience.

Once you have prepared the materials and set them out in the recommended positions, the children should be allowed to proceed independently (see photo above). Some children will almost completely avoid the pointed end. They might need a simple phrase of encouragement, such as "You can paint on the rest of the paper as you wish to." Whether or not they take your suggestion should be left entirely up to them.

To Cut Pennant Shapes

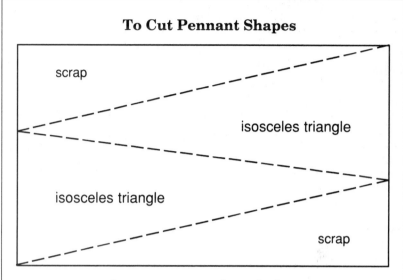

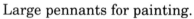

Large pennants for painting.

Small pennants for collage.

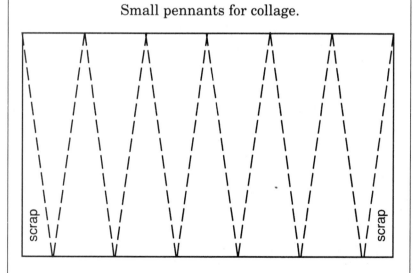

To Make a Rhythm Wand

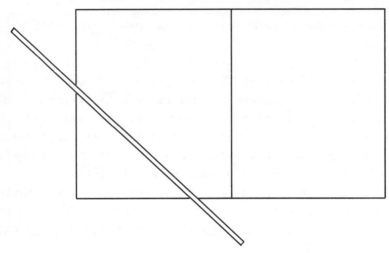

1. Place a ¼" wooden dowel 8" from the corner of an open sheet of newspaper.
2. Fold the corner over the dowel, and roll the paper tightly around the dowel to the opposite corner.

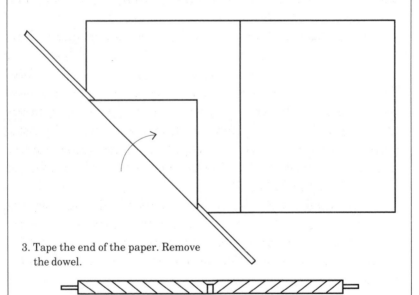

3. Tape the end of the paper. Remove the dowel.

Variations
- Pennants can be done on the floor, at a table, and on an easel or wall surface.
- Vary the color combinations of the paper and paints being used.
- Paint on rolls of paper approximately 12" wide, with the rolled end to the child's right. This encourages a left-to-right motion as the paper is unrolled to paint on—and on and on. The roll of paper should be on the floor and against a wall so that it can be unrolled only in one direction. The paint should be on a small tray kept at the child's left. (The tray is less apt to be moved to the right side than are individual cans.)
- Long, narrow strips of paper, for example—6" x 36"—can be used instead of the rolls or pennants. Again, by placing a tray of paints to the left of the paper, left-to-right movement can be encouraged.
- Provide long sticks or narrow boards, instructing the children to start at the left end and to continue until they reach the other end. Milk added to the paint will make it nearly waterproof; it won't come off on the children's hands when they hold the boards.
- To make *Rhythm Wands,* roll sheets of newspaper in long wands and paint them in a manner similar to the sticks or boards. See the diagram on page 148 for a good way to roll the newspaper. Be sure to add milk to the paint to make it more waterproof. With crepe paper or tissue paper streamers attached at the end, rhythm wands can be used for rhythmic creative movement activities, especially dancing and marching (see Cherry, *Creative Movement for the Developing Child,* Fearon Teacher Aids, 1971).
- To make *Rhythm Sticks,* roll newspaper in 11"–12" widths (see photo on p. 150) and have the children paint the rolls from left to right according to your directions. Be sure to add milk to the paint. The children can use these rhythm sticks for music activities.

Results

In painting on pennant-shaped papers or paper wands or sticks, children

1. *acquire an increased understanding of angles and triangles and may discover that triangles can have many different shapes and sizes,*
2. *enhance their creativity because the new paper shapes require new types of movements, especially the motion of working from left to right, which is the opposite of the way most young children who are right-handed usually work, and*
3. *enhance their awareness of how space can be divided.*

Making Rhythm Sticks.

NEGATIVE-SPACE PAINTINGS

Negative-space *Imagination Paper* can be used with many kinds of art activities, but it is especially interesting and developmental when used for painting. (See photo on p. 152.)

Prepare negative-space paper by cutting a hole in the paper to be painted on. The hole can be in the middle, on the side, near the top, near the bottom, or in a corner. It can be round, rectangular, oval, square, diamond-shaped, or any type of free-form shape, and it can be whatever size your imagination dictates. The first few times, the hole should be fairly simple. As the children become accustomed to the idea of painting around a hole, you can vary the shape of the paper any way you wish, and the simple cuts can become more complex.

Variations

• Use two or more cutout or torn spaces.
• Cut the paper in a geometric shape or in a free-form shape. But be cautious about the kinds of cuts you make around the border of the paper. Too big an inward cut or too sharp an angle is very difficult for preschool children to handle. They can handle free-form curved shapes very well.
• For *toddlers and two's* keep the paper simple and familiar. Use square, rectangular, round, or oval shapes for the holes. Cut only one hole in the paper. Many children under 3 will either ignore the hole totally and go on painting as though it weren't there, or they will paint the paper on only one side of the hole.

The first or second time a toddler or a 2-year-old, or even a 3-year-old, uses this type of paper, be sure to stand nearby to give reassurance if the child suddenly becomes aware that he or she is painting in the hole rather than on the paper around it. This is sometimes frightening to a child because of fear of wrongdoing. Should this occur, no explanation is needed. Simply smile, nod your head if it is natural for you to do so, and say, "That's all right. You're doing fine."

Negative-Space Painting. Peter (3¹/₂) is dealing effectively with the problem he encountered when painting on a sheet of paper with a hole in it.

Materials
Negative-space paper
Paints and brushes prepared as usual

Procedure
Negative-space paper should be placed directly on the paint board or easel, or a printed newspaper can be placed under a hole to make a more defined contrast for the child. Then simply allow the children to proceed as with any other painting.

If children say that there is a hole in the paper or that the paper is torn, simply tell them, "This is the only kind of paper we have today."

Some children will paint on only one side of the hole because of their inability to cross the midline (see p. 11). Sometimes children *will* cross the midline but will stay away from the negative space as much as possible—by going under it or to each side, but not next to it. Other children will outline the negative space or use it as the focal point for a design, a flower, or some other object. And still other children will copy the shape of the negative space (to the best of their ability) in one or more areas of the paper or, in some cases, scattered all over the paper.

Results
The use of negative-space paper helps children to
1. *develop problem-solving skills as they figure out how to deal with the space that is missing from their paper,*
2. *concentrate on the task, because they must keep their eyes on the paper and be aware of where they are moving the brush in order to avoid painting in the negative space,*
3. *improve their muscular coordination, because they need to give more specific direction to the brush to keep it from moving into the negative space,*
4. *intensify awareness of two-dimensional shapes and the division of space as they cope with both the shape of the paper and the shape of the negative space or spaces, and*
5. *learn that the "space that isn't there" may need to be given as much consideration as the space that is there, a concept that will be useful in later years as they become involved in abstract thinking and planning.*

MARKED IMAGINATION PAPER PAINTINGS

This project is similar to the previous one, except that instead of cutting or tearing holes in the paper, you provide the motivation by making crayon marks on the paper (see photo on p. 40). As with negative-space experiences, proceed slowly from a simple single mark to more complex marks. The mark might be one small circle or square, two such shapes, or a circle on one half of the paper and a rectangle on the other half. The marks can be very large, encompassing almost the entire sheet of paper, medium-sized, or very tiny. Use x's, lines, hearts, letters, numbers, and free-form shapes. Let your imagination be your guide.

Materials
Paper that has been marked with crayons (each paper may be marked differently)
Paints and brushes

Procedure
Allow children to select which paper they want and then to proceed with the painting in their own way. As with the negative-space paper, some children will simply go ahead as though there were no marks on the paper. Other children will avoid the marks or incorporate them into their designs. Sometimes children will copy the same kinds of marks with paint. And at other times they will deliberately try to cover the marks with the paint—although this is not always easy, because the crayons frequently bleed through.

Variations
• Make the marks with marking pens. They will be easy for the children to cover with paint.
• Make the marks by pasting on colored pieces of paper.
• Paste small pictures from a magazine on the paper instead of marking it with crayon.
• Rubber-stamp a picture on the paper rather than marking it with crayon.

Results
When using marked imagination paper, children may
   1. expand their imagination, stimulated by the color, shape, size, and placement of the marks,
   2. further develop problem-solving skills as they cope with the marks on their papers, and
   3. concentrate on the activity in order to utilize the marks in whatever way they have decided to do so.

OTHER KINDS OF PAINT

WATERCOLOR PAINTING

Children enjoy using watercolors especially when they are given good-quality, semimoist paint to work with. Watercolors are transparent with a sparkle that gives them a clean, fresh look. The colors are easily intermixed. The paint boxes, usually small and individual, are comfortable to use. They offer a satisfying change of pace for the child who has had many opportunities to work with tempera paints.

Watercolor paints are available in sets of four, six, eight, twelve, and sixteen colors. Because we use these paints with young children for experimentation and sensory training and not for the promotion of technical skills, I prefer to provide sets with at least eight colors.

This is a good time to make use of 9" x 12" white drawing paper, scraps of paper left over from larger cut sheets, and other odds and ends of paper accumulated over time. White paper should be used to take optimum advantage of the transparency of the paint.

Materials

Table and chairs (since watercolor painting is usually done while seated, although sometimes children want to paint while seated on the floor)

Paper in small sizes because the children's range of movement is confined to a smaller area than when they paint standing at a table or an easel

Water in a large can or jar for washing out the brushes—or two jars, one for washing the paint off the brush and the other for rinsing

Watercolors

Watercolor brushes of good quality (cheap brushes do not hold much water, thus diminishing the effect of using watercolors)

Greg and Alyce (both 4) apply watercolors to paper they have prepared by wrinkling it and dipping it in water. The colors blend together in unique patterns as they flow into the lines formed by the wrinkles.

Paper towels or a soft cloth on which to wipe the brushes after rinsing and before using a new color

Procedure

Show the children how to dip the brush in the water, wipe a little off on the edge of the container, and then dip only the point into the color desired.

Help the children learn to keep the brushes clean. This enables them to respond more freely to the paint, since the colors will remain bright and clear. Show them how to wipe the brush back and forth on the paper towel or cloth after rinsing it in the water.

Since the children are used to having a brush for each color when doing tempera painting, remind them of the importance of washing the brush thoroughly after each use.

Now allow the children the freedom to use the paint in their own way, as long as they follow the above guidelines.

Variations
- Wet the paper before applying the watercolor, thus allowing the colors to flow into one another.
- Watercolors are great for *Butterfly Blots,* described on pages 200–203.
- When the children have learned to care for the brush and the watercolors and to use them appropriately, provide high-quality professional watercolor paper. This is rather expensive, but you can cut the paper into small pieces, 6" x 9" or 8" x 10". The pebbly texture of the paper reflects the light and gives the colors an added brilliance.

Results
Painting with watercolors helps children to
1. *increase their aesthetic appreciation of all art because it increases their sensitivity to color, color mixtures, and color combinations,*
2. *develop fine motor control as they manipulate the movement of the brush on small sheets of paper in a limited working area,*
3. *learn to discriminate in selecting what color they will use next to another color,*
4. *practice following a sequence of directions as they learn about brush washing, care of the paints, and cleaning up,*
5. *heighten their self-confidence and self-esteem because of the ease with which they are able to transfer the colors from the pan to the paper, and*
6. *internalize a quality of aesthetic appreciation as they respond to the beauty of the pure colors.*

TEMPERA BLOCKS

A blending of tempera-painting and watercolor-painting techniques can be achieved through the use of tempera blocks. These are tempera paints that come in cakes of highly concentrated color. The average cake is approximately 1" thick and 2" in diameter (round) or 2" x 2½" (rectangular). The colors flow instantly from cake to wet brush, and, like watercolor paint, the colors intermix readily. Since the paint is opaque, rather than transparent, the pictorial effect is different from that of watercolors, and the children can paint over something they want to change.

Materials
Paper that is slightly larger than that used for watercolors, perhaps 9" x 12" to 12" x 18"
Water in containers as for watercolor
Brushes
Tempera blocks

Procedure
Follow the same procedure as with ordinary watercolors.

Results
In addition to the types of growth and learning that occur through other types of painting, the use of tempera blocks helps children to
1. *understand the difference between opaqueness and transparency,*
2. *gain in self-confidence as they are able to use the paints to go over something they already painted but want to change, and*
3. *respond to the brilliancy of the colors, resulting in an increased appreciation of aesthetic beauty.*

ADDING TEXTURES AND SCENTS TO PAINT

By adding various materials to the paint mixtures from time to time, the painting experience can be enriched in a wide variety of ways. You can decide whether you will do this before the children use the paint or whether they will add the materials.

Here are some ways in which you can add texture to paint.

To make one pint of tempera	*add small amounts of*
lumpy	flour (1 Tb.; don't stir much)
gritty	sand (1/2 tsp.)
slippery	glycerin (1 tsp.)
slimy	liquid soap that has become thick by standing uncovered for a week (2 Tb.)
sticky (dries shiny)	Karo syrup (2 Tb.)
shiny	Karo syrup (2 Tb.)
rough	fine sawdust (1 Tb.)
grainy (dries shiny)	sugar (1/2 cup)
sparkly (crystallizes when dry)	salt (1/2 cup; use various kinds, such as ice cream salt, kosher salt, epsom salt, and regular salt. Do not add salt too far in advance, because it dissolves quickly. Epsom salt, however, should be added several hours before use, in order to achieve full crystallization when it dries on the paper.)

OTHER ADDITIONS

Liquid soap or detergent added to the paint will make it possible to paint over crayon drawings or other waxy surfaces such as milk cartons, ice cream containers, and cottage cheese boxes. Add 1 Tb. of liquid soap to each pint of tempera. Too much soap added will give the paint a cloudy, dull cast when it dries.

Nontoxic wheat paste may be added to tempera in place of liquid soap or detergent to paint over waxy surfaces. Paint with wheat paste in it tends to be transparent, however. Adding white paint will make it more opaque.

SCENTS

Some days you may want to add something to your paint to change the odor. To half a pint of tempera, add any of the following items:

Cinnamon (1 tsp.)

Cloves (2 dozen)

Allspice (1 tsp.)

Cologne (2 Tb.)

Liquid food flavorings, such as vanilla, peppermint, chocolate, strawberry (1/2 tsp.)

Lemon juice (juice of one whole lemon)

Orange juice (juice of one whole orange)

MAKING PAINT FROM BASIC INGREDIENTS

An important part of the creative art experience is to give children an opportunity to prepare the paints themselves. The secret to this self-directed activity is to provide small quantities of materials. The value of the activity is in the complete trust given the children to handle the materials according to their abilities as they learn to create their own liquid tempera paint.

When children are making their own paint (or engaged in any other self-directed activity), it is best to have no more than three working together in any one area (see p. 265).

Materials

Small clear plastic drinking glasses, each with 1 tablespoon of powdered tempera

Tongue depressors or plastic or wooden spoons to use for scooping out and mixing the paint

A small container of water

Eyedroppers for measuring out the water

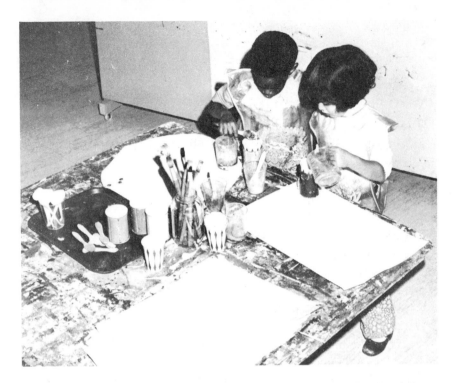

Brandon and Connie (both 4) are completely absorbed in the task of mixing their own tempera paint.

3-oz. paper cups in which to mix the paints (the small size will limit the amount of materials each child uses)

Notes to fasten to each painting that say, "We are very proud that your child made the liquid tempera paint used in this picture. It was very hard. Ask him or her about it."

Procedure

Set all the materials in the middle of the table where the children will be working so that they have to reach forward to take the items they want. The children use 3-oz. cups to mix only enough paint for themselves (the cups are thrown away after the project is finished).

As the photograph above shows, the children place their 3-oz. paper cups into stronger 5-oz. cups to make them easier to hold without crushing. In the photograph, a child is pouring water into the paint. This usually results in too much water, however, so it is better to add the water with an eyedropper. The children should stir the paint with a spoon or a stick rather than with a brush because stirring can damage the bristles.

Once the paint is mixed, the children use it to create a painting.

Variations
• Water can also be dispensed from empty hand-lotion bottles or other bottles that have a built-in dispenser top.
• See *Paint-making Experiments* (pp. 163–165) for additional variations.

How Children Approach This Project
When children make their own paint, they are sometimes so proud of a color they have mixed that they may cover an entire paper with a wash of that one color. Or when they have mixed several colors, they may keep the line where one color meets another very distinct, taking care not to let one of their great colors run into another. This extra care to keep the colors separate frequently results in more deliberate designs and color patterns than when the children are using ready-mixed paint.

Results
In exploring the connections between motor and cognitive development, I have experimented with the effects of children stirring with a circular motion and have found that such a motion contributes to increased facility with and enunciation of words (Cherry, Creative Play for the Developing Child, *Fearon Teacher Aids, 1976, p. 191). The carry-over lasts from approximately five to twenty minutes.*

In addition, paint-making will help children to

1. *sharpen eye-hand coordination and overall visual motor coordination skills,*
2. *develop concepts of quantity and proportion as they discover that adding more water makes the paint thinner and lighter in color,*

These 4- and 5-year-olds, with the help of a visiting father, are adding kitchen cleanser, toothpaste, hand lotion, and liquid soap to liquid tempera. They will compare their mixtures and discuss the results. The discoveries they make during this activity are especially important because they are *their own*.

3. *develop concepts of time as they discover that some colors need to be stirred for a longer time than others in order to dissolve,*
4. *increase feelings of self-esteem as an understanding develops of the ability to both make and control materials, and*
5. *enhance awareness of color and color patterns as the color and texture of the newly made paint takes on new importance. This awareness is then transferred to art work with other media.*

PAINT-MAKING EXPERIMENTS

After children have had considerable experience painting with tempera, give them opportunities to experiment with creating various new mixtures to use as paint. Instead of using paint with ingredients added by the teacher, in this project the children mix the additions into the paint in an exploratory manner.

Materials
 Several containers of paint to be shared
 Medium-sized pieces of painting paper
 Stiff-bristle brushes that can be used for mixing and painting
 Disposable muffin tins with four sections, or eight-section
  tins cut in half, or containers such as small jars or empty
  cottage cheese cartons
 Several ingredients to try, one at a time, to mix with the paint
  (the children may suggest others besides the suggestions
  below)

Addition	*Possible Result*
Canned milk	Hard, washable finish
Toothpaste	Transparent; easy to mix; smells good
Face cream	Greasy; does not mix
Hand cream	Hard to mix, but can be done with persistent effort
Hand lotion	Good smell; semitransparent
Liquid soap (old and thickened)	Slimy; very transparent
Kitchen cleanser	Powdery when dry; opaque; dull
Salad oil	Does not mix; oily
Catsup	Nauseating to adults, but fun for children; catsup smell
Mustard	Nauseating to adults, but fun for children; mustard smell
Rice	Gritty
Shaving cream	Creamy; smells good

Procedure
Place all materials in the center of the working area. A lazy
susan is ideal for this type of activity.
 Allow several children to select a color of paint and place a
little in each section of a muffin tin (or other container).

The children then select four ingredients to add to their four colors of paint. Only one ingredient is added to each color. Stress the use of a circular stirring motion when mixing the ingredient into the color.

After trying each mixture on paper, the children who are working together and the adult facilitator discuss the results as a group. Because the discussion is an important aspect of this activity, it calls for closer supervision than do most other art projects.

After some experimentation with several types of mixtures, have the children each pick their favorite mixtures with which to create a painting.

Variations
- Go for a walk with the children around the school building and find things that might make a good experiment in paint mixing.
- Have children mix two ingredients in one paint color.
- Prepare a group sampler, with each child using a different ingredient and applying a different mixture to the same picture.

Results
This experimental paint-mixing project helps children to
  1. *acquire experience in experimentation and planning,*
  2. *expand their ability to discriminate between various odors, textures, and effects,*
  3. *increase their ability to judge quantities,*
  4. *intensify their small motor control as they control the amounts of ingredients added to the paint,*
  5. *further develop their stirring ability, which can increase their facility with and enunciation of words (as mentioned on p. 162), and*
  6. *verbalize their observations and their summation of an experience.*

WHIPPED SOAP

Whipped-soap paint can be made with either mild laundry soap or powdered or liquid detergent. Soap retains the color in the foam better than detergent, so it is much more satisfactory. Soap is also easier to clean up. Soap flakes, if they are available, result in a better texture than does powdered soap.

Materials

A pitcher of water of a size the children can easily handle
A container to mix the soap in
A hand-operated eggbeater
Soap powder or flakes
Food coloring
Paper on which to paint
Brushes, sponges, and other painting tools if desired
(see pp. 193–195)

Procedure

The children can each make their own paint, or they can do it as a group activity to conserve materials.

A little water is poured into the container. Soap is added, a little at a time. The soap and water are stirred gently with a spoon. The eggbeater is used to whip the mixture until it gets frothy, but not too stiff.

Caution: If whipped until stiff, the mixture will probably be too slippery to adhere to most papers. If too much soap is added or if the mixture is mixed even fairly stiff, it will crack on the paper after drying.

After the soap is whipped, color can be added gradually and mixed by hand. The resultant colors will be very pale.

Variations

• Without color added, whipped soap can be used for the effect of snow on individual paintings or on a group mural or other projects.
• Whipped paint can be used for decorative borders and de-

Mark and Terri (both 5) make whipped soap paint while Jaqui and Jo-Jo (both 4½) watch.

signs on painted boxes or other containers.
- Apply the whipped paint with a sponge for extra decorative effects.

Results

This activity of adding soap to liquid and then whipping it may help children to

1. *expand their ability to measure and to judge quantities,*
2. *increase their scientific knowledge as they watch the mixture becoming frothy and then hardening after being applied to paper and allowed to dry,*
3. *heighten aesthetic awareness as they become involved with the very delicate pastel tints they create, and*
4. *develop motor skills because the operation of the eggbeater requires a rotary movement—which will involve the wrist if the child is over age 2 or 2½.*

MOOD PAINTINGS

The key to effective, creative teaching is to watch for clues in the behavior of the children and then to respond to those clues in ways that will benefit them. Moods are important keys to understanding others as individuals.

Notice how different children move when handling various materials. Watch for changes in their facial expressions as they go through the various processes of each project. Look for excitement or boredom or anticipation or apprehension as they experiment with new materials and new procedures. Share their pride in their growing ability to manipulate tools, and cushion their disappointment when they lose control. Try to recognize their varied emotional needs and their changing moods and realize that art experiences are excellent for helping to release one's tensions.

In addition to your observations, help the children to know and understand moods. Tell them that everyone has feelings and that our feelings create our moods. Let them know that in art they should feel free to express their own moods.

Experiment with *Mood Paintings*. These will help children understand what moods are and to talk about them. (See also pp. 251–252 for Mood Collages.)

SUNNY DAY MOOD PAINTINGS

Materials

A variety of light colors of paper for the background
A selection of light colors of paints, with brushes

Procedure

This project should be done with a group of four to six children at a time so that each one has an opportunity to fully explore his or her feelings with you.

Discuss the sun and how it makes us feel. If it is a sunny day, walk outdoors and feel the warmth of the sun.

Ask the children to pick out the colors of paint and paper that make them feel like the sun.

Allow them to proceed independently, and encourage them to verbalize their feelings as they paint.

When they are finished, have each child describe the feelings he or she experienced and try to establish what type of mood was developed.

FOGGY DAY MOOD PAINTINGS

Materials

Black, white, and gray paint

Large brushes

A variety of colors of paper, especially gray, blue, and white

Procedure

Discuss which kind of paper makes the black and white paint look most like a foggy day.

Discuss how foggy days feel. What kinds of moods do they put us in?

Allow children to proceed and experiment on their own, as you encourage them to verbalize their feelings.

HAPPY MOOD PAINTINGS

Materials

Newspapers

White paint

A variety of other colors of paint

A 2" varnish brush, so that a large area can be covered with one stroke

A variety of other brushes and other painting tools

Procedure

Have the children each paint a sheet of newspaper with the white paint.

While the paint is drying, discuss happy moods. Talk about things that make us laugh. Talk about jokes, clowns, and other funny things. Ask the children if they like funny things. Would they like to be a clown? Why? Are clowns always happy? Do they prefer being happy or sad?

When the newspaper is dry, ask the children to proceed any way they wish to make a *Happy Mood Painting*.

Have children who are 5 years old and older paint a happy or sad clown face.

NIGHT MOOD PAINTINGS

Materials

Materials suggested by the children (see Procedure, below)

Stars, glitter, and other sparkly things, with the appropriate adhesive materials for them

Procedure

After doing the other mood projects, perhaps over the course of a couple of weeks, tell the children you want them to paint pictures of night moods.

Have the children tell you what materials to provide them with.

All of the suggestions should be discussed as a group and then modified to suit your own mood and the general tenor of the group.

Encourage the children to proceed according to their own ideas.

Variations for Mood Paintings

• Use sponges instead of brushes.
• Apply the paint with cotton balls.

- Pre-select the colors, for example, light blue paper and yellow, light orange, yellow orange, and white paint for *Sunny Day Mood Paintings.*

Results
Mood paintings, when accompanied by periods of free discussion, help children to
  1. *learn to verbalize their feelings and*
  2. *learn to express their feelings and moods through legitimate outlets.*

COMMUNICATION THROUGH PAINTINGS

Young children do not *need* to be given subject matter to paint. The painting materials and the manner in which they are presented are motivation enough. As the children experiment with and react to the wide variety of materials you have offered, they develop concepts of color, balance, rhythm, and design— all of which are crucial to the development of true creative skills. They learn to sense just where to put the next brush stroke, the contrasting color, the curved line. They may select the color that is closest, or they may carefully pick out colors that reflect their mood or their innate and developing sense of design.

Paintings by young children communicate much in the way of feelings, expression, and reaction to the environment. The children sense this communication as they note the expression on a parent's face when the newest painting is brought home, or as they note the care with which you mount and display the newest painting. If the activities have been appropriate to the children's various levels of ability and if the children have been allowed to pursue the activities freely, then they will have each grown richer in all areas of development—especially in the ability to communicate without words.

THE NEXT STEP: REPRESENTATIONAL PAINTINGS

Five-year-old children begin to develop the desire to communicate through representational paintings. You may then occasionally want to suggest some subject matter that relates to a class activity, a field trip, a story or poem, or some aspect of the child's own imagination.

Caution must be taken only to *encourage,* and not to direct. To inspire artistic achievement and communication is your task; to discover their own creative abilities is the task of the children. They must be allowed to *represent things in their own way, with their own ideas of perspective.* Children must be allowed to move at *their own pace and in their own individual style.* If the motivation you give takes some children off into unexpected tangents, applaud their originality and appreciate their ability for self-direction. Listen to the children and learn about the unexpected ways of their imaginations. This is creativity. Listen to them and allow your own creative self to grow.

CHAPTER 7

Painting with Fingers, Feather Dusters, and Other Tools

The teacher keeps telling me to keep my hands out of the paint. Even when it's my paint on my paper, she says, "No, no, not with your fingers. Use your brush." But now she's given me this really big piece of paper and a jar of paint. She wet the paper with a sponge and told me I can take the orange paint (it looks like paste) and smear it all over the paper.

OK. Here goes. Feels gishy—and mushy—and oh—oh— oh—I like it. She says I can use both hands. Oh, look, I go 'round and 'round and it leaves my finger marks all over. See! See! Look at what the end of my fist does when I go 'round and 'round.

Ohhhh! Here's some red magenta paint. I'll take a goop of that and smear it on top of the orange. How be-a-u-ti-ful! "Teacher, teacher. Look what I made." Oh, I like this. I'm going around and around and up and down. See! See! See my finger marks. That's me.

I'm a me!

FINGERPAINTING

Smearing mixtures with their fingers is not a new experience for most children, but by the time they reach a preschool group, it has become a repressed art. When fingerpainting is presented to them as a school experience, they frequently approach it with great caution. They do not quite understand why, after being told many times to keep their hands clean and to wash them with soap, the teacher is now encouraging them to get their hands dirty.

With children who continue to balk, be very patient and gentle and give them plenty of time to decide to participate. A small amount of a very light color of fingerpaint, such as yellow, added to liquid soap, can help to convince children that they will not be punished for fingerpainting. Once they hear the word *soap,* their fears are usually lessened, because their mothers like soap. Usually only one or two such experiences are necessary before a reluctant child is ready to use the regular fingerpaints like the other children.

PREPARATION

Fingerpainting should be done while standing at a table. The table should be low enough (14" to 18" or 20") to encourage movement of the entire body as it picks up the rhythm of the arm and hand activity. Enough space should be allowed to ensure that one child's movements do not interfere with the freedom of those of another child.

Provide aprons for teachers and children.

Place protective coverings on areas where they are needed.

Have a bucket or a dishpan of soapy water nearby so that the children can rinse their hands before going through the classroom or the halls to wash them at a sink. Place paper towels nearby for hand drying and for emergency cleanups. Kitchen sponges are also useful.

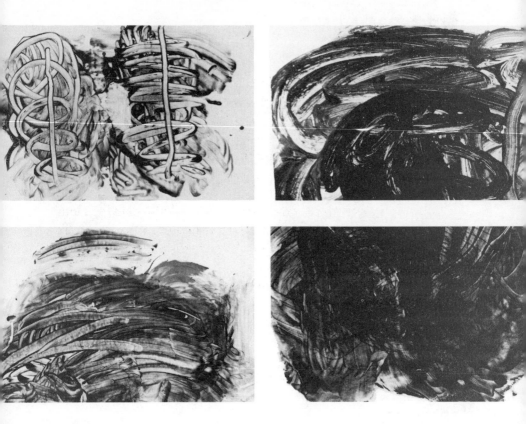

Fingerpainting. There is considerable variation and individuality in these finger-paintings as well as evidence of a developing sense of rhythm, balance, and symmetry, indicating that the children are learning to function in a bilateral manner. Fingerpainting is one of the most important types of art experience for young children. It has a wholesome influence in the affective and cognitive areas of their development.

PAPER

For fingerpainting, I prefer a heavy butcher paper to most fingerpaint papers, because butcher paper is usually of better quality. You can also try good drawing paper, at least 60-lb. weight but preferably 80-lb., although that is quite expensive. You can also try waterproof wallpaper, plastic-coated drawer-lining or shelf paper, or a smooth-finished cardboard, such as tagboard. Whatever you use, remember that it must have a smooth surface.

Some teachers spray the paper with a light coat of clear plastic to make their own high-quality fingerpaint paper. To keep the paper from curling as it dries, fold under each edge of each sheet of paper about 1 inch.

Wet the fingerpaint paper before using it. Dipping the paper in water or wetting the table with a sponge before putting the paper down and then sponging the paper are two common methods. Wetting the surface underneath the paper prevents slipping. If liquid starch or liquid soap is used for the paint media, however, the surface of the table does not need to be wet in advance.

PAINT

Some commercially prepared fingerpaint should be kept on hand. It is usually very effective. You can also prepare your own fingerpaint by adding liquid tempera, commercial finger-paint, or food coloring to cooked or liquid starch, wheat paste, library paste, or even liquid soap or buttermilk. Be cautioned that the tendency is to add too much color, thus making the paint too opaque for a successful fingerpaint experience. Remember that *transparency* is the key.

Fingerpaints are also more effective when used sparingly; this allows the finger marks to show through. Provide small spoons for scooping up small amounts of paint. The spoons must always be replaced in their original containers.

Materials
   Fingerpaint in shallow containers
   Small spoons
   Large sheets of good-quality painting paper or fingerpaint
      paper

Procedure
A simple suggestion, such as "You may cover the whole paper if you like," may encourage children to start fingerpainting. Allow them to move their hands as they wish, although you may want to suggest, "You may use your whole hand if you wish." As children become more experienced, they should be encouraged to use the entire hand.

Variations
• Play recorded music while the children are fingerpainting. Remind them to listen to the music. Most will move to the rhythm. Just quietly make a mental note of those who don't. Not moving to the music may be a clue about a possible hearing or auditory-perceptual problem. For more on musical fingerpainting, see pages 185–188.
• Add liquid starch or buttermilk to commercial fingerpaint to make a mixture that children can pour instead of spoon onto the paper. Such a mixture can be put into small pitchers or bottles that the children can handle without adult assistance.
• Use small salt shakers filled with tempera powder to sprinkle over liquid starch or buttermilk for another type of experience. Be sure to use small shakers to avoid powder dust. (The blue color of the liquid starch may alter the tempera colors somewhat, especially white, yellow, orange, and red.)
• Make *Sticky Fingerpaintings* by adding a very small amount of Karo syrup to the mixture, or pour a little syrup directly onto the paper to be blended in by the child during the painting process.

- Make *Gooey Fingerpaintings* by putting a spoonful of vegetable glue onto the paper next to the fingerpaint.
- Make *Lumpy Fingerpaintings* by adding a little lumpy flour-and-water mixture to the paint.
- Make *Sandy Fingerpaintings* by adding a little sand to the paint.
- Make *Textured Fingerpaintings* by painting on textured paper. Have children prepare their own textured paper by pasting a variety of torn paper shapes all over a sheet of paper.
- Make *Combed Fingerpaintings* by using a pocket comb to create a design on the fingerpaint. Or prepare cardboard combs by cutting teeth of different widths into a piece of sturdy cardboard.

Mary (4) and Tom (5) introduce fingerpainting to their brother, Stephen (2). In creative developmental art, children are always able to help younger children because each child learns the basic procedures required for each activity.

- Make *Object Fingerpaintings* by giving the children a variety of small objects with which they can create designs on the paint. These objects can be jar lids, bottle caps, pen covers, paper clips, and similar small items. Limit the number of objects, and provide them only after the children have spread the fingerpaint manually for a while, and then only if they want to experiment with additional possibilities.
- Make *Crayon Fingerpaintings* by painting over paper that has been previously covered with crayons. The crayon underneath the fingerpaint produces a luminous effect.

Results
When children participate in fingerpaint experiences, they
1. *reawaken within themselves early tactile memories that they have been forced to repress,*
2. *intensify their visual perception skills,*
3. *heighten their kinesthetic awareness through direct physical interaction with the material,*
4. *develop ego strength, which leads to increased social confidence, as they learn how easily they can control the paint,*
5. *internalize concepts of color and transparency,*
6. *expand their awareness of the potential for rhythmic movement as they respond to the accompanying music and rhythms,*
7. *strengthen their developing sensorimotor skills, and*
8. *are provided with avenues for the free expression of feelings and healthy emotional release.*

PUDDING PAINTING

Pudding Painting should be offered to children at least once during a school year. Instead of paint, prepare a large quantity of several flavors of pudding. Add some whipped cream if you wish. Use a clean plastic covering or table top to paint on. Suggest that the painting be limited to the palms of the hands and fingers. When finished, the children can lick the pudding off of themselves.

MUD PAINTING

Add some liquid soap and liquid starch to mud to increase its transparency. First try it out on paper. After some experience with the mud mixture, have children fingerpaint on the outside of a window that can later be washed with a hose.

Variation

• Make mud handprints on the outside of a window.

MONOPRINTS

These are prints that result on a sheet of paper that is placed over a fingerpainting and patted down.

Materials

Tempera paint with a very small amount of glycerin added
A plastic board, cloth, or table top
Good-quality drawing paper

Procedure

Allow the children to paint freely on the plastic surface.

Place a sheet of drawing paper over the painting momentarily. Pat the surface lightly. Remove the paper with a quick, upward motion to keep from changing the design by smearing it.

Variation

• Allow a monoprint in one color to dry thoroughly. Then make another monoprint on the same paper with a contrasting color. Continue the procedure with different combinations of colors.

Results
In addition to the general results of fingerpainting already outlined, monoprints enable children to
1. *expand their concepts of reversibility and*
2. *heighten their feelings of anticipation as they await the outcome.*

FOOTPAINTING
Footpainting can be an interesting warm-weather experiment and is an excellent exercise for building body image.

Materials
 Large sheets of paper spread on the floor
 Buttermilk with small quantities of liquid tempera added
 Soapy water and towels for clean up after the activity
 Low chairs for children to sit in

Procedure
Have children sit on the chairs as they spread the buttermilk-paint mixture around on the paper. The surface will be very slippery, so the children should not stand up.

Variations
• Footprints can be made by using paint only on the bottom of the feet. Hold on to the children's hands as they walk the length of the paper with the paint on their feet.
• While sitting in a chair, each child makes a *Butterfly Print* by crossing the feet so that the left foot is on the right side and the right foot is on the left side. The resulting image looks somewhat like a butterfly. But more important, the children can challenge adults to tell them what is "wrong" with the picture. It takes most people a little time to realize that the footprints are reversed.
• The children can also make *Reversed Handprints* in a similar

Organic Fingerpainting. Julie and Ian (both 4) are experimenting with adding salad oil, liquid starch, wheat paste, hand lotion, and shaving cream to their fingerpaint. They are free to use these materials in their own way.

manner. The result will look as though the print had been made by the back of the hand.

Results
These activities help children to
1. *increase their sensory awareness,*
2. *release the remnants of any inhibitions stemming from early repressions of messy activities,*
3. *enhance self-awareness and body image, and*
4. *invent imaginative use of media.*

ORGANIC FINGERPAINTING

Organic Fingerpainting is a very effective basic learning experience.

Materials

A variety of "paints" in their original containers, including liquid starch, library paste, hand lotion, vegetable glue, shaving cream in an aerosol can, cooked starch, dry wheat paste, cake flour, baking soda, baking powder, cocoa, salad oil, buttermilk, canned milk, and similar materials (let your imagination guide you in discovering new ingredients to use)

Small pitchers of water

Tempera paint in small containers

Eyedroppers for dropping the paint onto the paper

Paper, as for other fingerpaint projects

Procedure

Allow children to select the colors and as many ingredients as they wish and to use them mixed together as in traditional fingerpainting.

Results

As the children indulge in this exploratory project, they

1. *develop trust in others as they sense the teachers trust them,*
2. *experience the result of their own choices and actions,*
3. *internalize concepts of basic scientific principles, such as transparency, stickiness, oiliness, smoothness, absorbency, ability to blend, and opaqueness,*
4. *increase self-confidence as they experience the freedom of choice that accompanies this type of activity, and*
5. *increase their ability to withstand the emotional pressures of highly structured situations they encounter in other areas of their lives.*

SHAVING CREAM FINGERPAINTING

Using shaving cream as a fingerpaint medium is a favorite activity of mine, stemming from the fact that a child invented it. Many years ago an area had been set up to play barber shop, complete with cardboard razors and shaving cream in aerosol cans. Nearby a fingerpainting activity was going on. Tanya, 4, on impulse grabbed some shaving cream from the other center, sprayed it on her paper, and blithely began to paint with it, thus starting an entire new trend.

Use shaving cream, preferably scented (but avoid menthol scents). Provide a smooth-topped table on which to do the painting.

One-third cup of water will keep the shaving cream from becoming too dry. Sometimes a small amount of paint can be added to the shaving cream when it is on the table.

Although I don't always use musical accompaniment for fingerpainting, I almost always do when the children paint with shaving cream.

Have two or three pieces of stiff cardboard handy to use to push the leftover fingerpaint to one area for cleanup when the activity is over.

FINGERPAINTING TO MUSIC

Fingerpainting is a rhythmic movement experience, and it can be enhanced through the use of music. Once the children have become thoroughly familiar with fingerpaint and have had plenty of time to explore its possibilities and develop their individual styles, music can add a completely new dimension.

Because any rhythmic movement activity should be based on children's natural movements, it is important that they be able to work with the materials on their own terms and with their own types of movements before they perform the activity with musical accompaniment.

Types of Music
Start with lively waltzes, such as "The Skater's Waltz" or "The Blue Danube." Then try a folk dance, such as "Round and Round the Village" or "Way Down Yonder in the Paw-Paw Patch." Most children prefer fast music, and they like it loud.

Fingerpainting to Music. Cooked starch, a choice of dry or liquid tempera, and an oversized piece of butcher paper fastened to the ends of the table give Jamie (4) an opportunity for full arm movements as he fingerpaints to music. This experience lasted 20 minutes.

But do give them opportunities to move to slow, quiet music, such as "Are You Sleeping, Brother John?" or some lullabies. Even old classics such as "Moonlight Sonata" or "Red River Valley" provide appropriate fingerpaint accompaniment.

Procedure

Set out fingerpaint materials as usual. Turn on the music. Tell the children they can rinse off their hands whenever they want to, dance a while to the music, then go back to their painting and move their arms to the music.

Use a tambourine for accompaniment as you improvise songs. Soon the children will help you with the singing. Here are some of my favorites, sung to familiar tunes.

1. Try the following lyrics to the tune of "Skip to My Lou."

My hands slide over the paper two by two.
My hands slide over the paper two by two.
My hands slide over the paper two by two.
Skip to my Lou, my darling.
I can make a motion; so can you.
I can make a motion; so can you.
I can make a motion; so can you.
Skip to my Lou, my darling.
Now I'll do another one; you can do it, too.
Now I'll do another one; you can do it, too.
Now I'll do another one; you can do it, too.
Skip to my Lou, my darling.
(Continue singing, with the children making up new verses.)

2. Try this song, "Ten Little Fingers," to the tune of "Ten Little Indians," with shaving cream.
   One little, two little, three little fingers,
   Four little, five little, six little fingers,
   Seven little, eight little, nine little fingers,
   Ten little fingerpaint marks.
   Five little fingers on each hand now,
   Two little hands that I have somehow,
   A wrist, and back of hand, and even an elbow,
   Make little fingerpaint marks.

3. "Go In and Out the Window" doesn't need any change of words. I recommend doing this song as the children move around the table while fingerpainting, especially during the first verse.
   Go 'round and 'round the village.
   Go 'round and 'round the village.
   Go 'round and 'round the village,
   As we have done before.
   Go in and out the window.

Go in and out the window.
Go in and out the window,
As we have done before.
Now stand and face your partner.
(Children can gently rub fingerpainted hands with one another.)
Now stand and face your partner.
Now stand and face your partner,
As we have done before.
(Repeat first verse.)

Results
Fingerpainting to music will help children to
1. *sharpen their auditory-perceptual and visual-motor abilities,*
2. *improve their overall muscular control,*
3. *develop bilateral integration of both sides of the body,*
4. *experience a release of tension as they react to the kinesthetic sensations produced by the blending of fingerpaint media, paper, movement, and music, and*
5. *increase their ability to plan their own use of space and movements in order to give consideration to the space and movements of others.*

OTHER WAYS TO PAINT WITHOUT BRUSHES

PAINTING WITH SPONGES
Sponges of all types and sizes encourage experimentation with textural effects.

Materials
Household or natural sponges
Snap clothespins for holding the sponges

Shallow containers with about ⅛" to ¼" of paint
White drawing or painting paper, or construction paper in
   colors that contrast with the paint colors being used

Procedure
Clip a clothespin to a sponge or a piece of sponge and dip it into
the paint. Apply the color to the paper with the sponge.

Variations
• Use small pieces of sponge to decorate tissue paper for gift
  wrap.
• Use large, flat sponges for crisscrossing shapes over one
  another across a large piece of paper.
• Use sponges dipped in white paint over a crayoned scribble
  design.
• Use sponges dipped in pastel paint over a crayoned scribble
  design.
• Use sponges over a brush painting.

Results
Experimenting with sponge painting helps children to
   1. increase their knowledge of textural qualities,
   2. increase their awareness of transparency and overlap,
   3. explore creatively, and
   4. develop motor control as they learn to adjust the pres-
      sure of the sponge to achieve different effects.

PAINTING WITH FEATHER DUSTERS

I first introduced the use of feather dusters as a painting tool
at a Head Start art workshop during the 1960s. Early childhood teachers now universally use feather dusters as a means
of exploring color and space with paint, and this has led to the
exploration, by myself and others, of the potential of many
other household and natural materials as painting tools.

Feather dusters are generally obtainable in grocery stores or any other store that carries household supplies.

They can be used over and over again. Wash them gently after each use. Shake them gently, wrap them in a towel to blot them, and lay them out to finish drying naturally, preferably in the sunshine.

Since they are made of a natural material, feather dusters will deteriorate if stored for too long a time in a very dry place. You can tell that this is happening if the feathers come out easily. The dusters should then be discarded.

Materials

Feather dusters (one for each color of paint)
Pie tins
Paint
Recorded music (optional)

Procedure

The paint should be fairly thick to minimize its splashing over the surrounding area. The paint should be spread thinly on the bottom of the container so that primarily the tips of the feathers get wet. Encourage the children to paint lightly with the feather dusters in order to try to achieve a feathery effect. The children will probably be more interested, however, in the large areas they can cover at one time than in the quality of the strokes.

Play music occasionally for the children to paint to.

Variations

• Instead of paint, use liquid starch with powdered paint over it. The starch and paint mix together as the child dips the feather duster in the container.
• Instead of individual pie tins, use one large cake pan or, even better, a disposable aluminum baking pan. Pour some liquid starch in two diagonally opposite corners of the pan and in the center. Sprinkle each pool of starch with powdered

Painting with a feather duster enables Dani (3) to cover his paper quickly with little muscular effort.

tempera, using colors that will blend harmoniously when they are intermingled with one another.

- Provide a large pan as above, placing liquid paint in the corners and center instead of the starch and powdered paint.
- Provide a separate feather duster with a very small amount of black paint, which can be "feathered" over a completed painting.
- Provide a paper for a large mural. Several children can work on it at one time, and several shifts can take turns. Use several pure colors of paint. When the paper has been solidly covered, continue to use the same colors with *white* added. The pastel colors are complemented by the darker background colors. (The cover painting is an example.)
- When doing a mural, as above, put out a duster with white or with black (instead of pastel colors) after much of the paper has already been covered.

Results

The use of feather dusters (and other household brushes) as painting tools is an exhilarating experience for children as they

1. *greatly increase their temporal awareness when they discover they are able to cover the paper very quickly,*
2. *grow in self-esteem as they observe their power and the results of their actions,*
3. *develop a greater understanding of motor control as they move to the rhythm of the accompanying music, utilizing the large spaces of paper, and*
4. *extend their ability to understand cause and effect as they realize they are able to cover a large expanse of paper with minimal muscular exertion.*

PAINTING WITH TWO FEATHER DUSTERS

This excellent rhythmic exercise uses two feather dusters instead of one, and the painting is done to the accompaniment of music.

Materials

One feather duster for each hand
Paint (one color for each duster)
Large sheets of paper mounted on a wall
Musical accompaniment

Procedure

Apply the paint to the paper using both feather dusters while moving to the rhythm of the music.

Variations

• Use one color of paint for both feather dusters.
• Place the paper higher up so that the children will need to stretch to paint on it.
• Place the paper on the floor so that the children will have to

paint in a bent-over position while moving to the music. (See also "Arm Dancing," pp. 83–85.)

Results
This experience will help children to
  1. *further develop their ability to function bilaterally as they use both sides of their bodies at once and*
  2. *increase visual-motor perception and eye-hand coordination as they follow their arm movements while reaching and stretching.*

PAINTING WITH FEATHERS
Individual feathers can be used for painting, as a follow-up to feather duster painting.

Materials
  Feathers (instead of paintbrushes)
  Tempera paint that has been thinned to a lighter consistency than normal
  Paper, not larger than 18" x 24" and preferably smaller

Procedure
Allow the children to explore this painting tool on their own.

Results
When painting with single feathers, children will
  1. *improve their ability to make comparisons as they note differences between using one feather and using a feather duster,*
  2. *strengthen motor control as they sense the difference of muscular exertion needed when only one feather is used, and*
  3. *internalize concepts of delicacy.*

PAINTING WITH TWIGS, BRANCHES, AND OTHER GROWING THINGS

Collect an assortment of as many different kinds of twigs and small leafy branches as you can. Search out trees and bushes of many varieties. For example, you might collect a small twig from a pine tree with several bunches of pine needles on it, a twig from a pepper tree, and a small branch off a bottlebrush bush. Enlist the aid of your students. Ask for their parents' help. Once you have a small assortment, proceed as follows.

Materials
One or more types of twigs, leaves, or branches
Paint, prepared similarly to that used with feather dusters (described above)
Large sheets of drawing or painting paper

Procedure
Allow children to experiment in their own way.

Variations
• Use very thick, creamy paint.
• Use very thin paint.
• Use very small twigs and stems with leaves on them.
• Use with very small sheets of paper.
• Use green paint on white paper. Use varying shades of green. Sometimes apply it to green paper.
• Use black paint on green paper.
• Use light green paint on black paper.
• After a twig or leaf painting is finished, use cutouts of small pieces of sponge, with clothespin holders, to make "flowers" on the design.

Results
Using objects from nature as painting tools enables children to

1. *become more aware of nature and growing things, as they experience them in a new way,*
2. *increase their textural awareness,*
3. *increase their concepts of likenesses and differences, and*
4. *develop an awareness of aesthetics as they observe the natural beauty of some of the marks they make.*

PAINTING WITH COTTON SWABS

A cotton swab is good to use when you have a short session and want an activity that will be easy to prepare and easy to clean up afterward.

Materials

Q-Tips (or other brand of cotton-tipped sticks)
A divided container, such as an egg carton, with a small amount of tempera paint in each section
Small pieces of paper, cardboard, or cloth

Procedure

Allow the children to experiment as they wish.

Results

Using this small paint tool, especially if it is used after the large ones described above, helps children to

1. *internalize the difference between large and small,*
2. *realize there are many ways to achieve similar goals,*
3. *appreciate that it is their work with the paint that makes the picture, not the tool they use,*
4. *develop fingertip control, which is required by the small circumference of the cotton swab, and*
5. *internalize the concept of absorbency as they note that the cotton absorbs the paint and they may have to redip it two or three times to get a workable amount of paint.*

PAINTING WITH SPRAY BOTTLES

Spray bottles can be obtained from a variety of household products such as soaps, lotions, and window cleaners. Before using them for paints, clean the bottles thoroughly with a bleach solution to remove completely all hazardous residue.

Select only those bottles that children can operate easily with their little fingers. Some spray bottles may be too difficult for them to handle.

Materials

Spray bottles

Tempera mixed to a thin enough consistency to spray easily

Large sheets of paper, cardboard, or other surfaces that can be painted on

Procedure

Allow children to experiment with the effects of spraying various colors on top of one another.

Variations

- Spray light colors on dark papers, and dark colors on light papers.
- Use spray paints over a feather duster painting (pp. 189–192).
- Spray only dark colors over much of the paper's surface. Then exchange dark colors for light ones.
- Reverse the above procedure, spraying the paper with light colors and then spraying dark colors over the light ones.

Results

The use of spray bottles to apply paint will enable children to

1. expand their awareness of cause and effect,

2. give important exercise to finger and fingertip muscles, the last part of the hands to develop, and

3. enhance creative planning skills as they realize the unique effects they can obtain with different types of spray techniques, color combinations, and textures.

Three different types of paint rollers and three different colors of paint provide Carole (4) with a challenging experience.

PAINTING WITH ROLLERS

Painting with rollers is closely akin to sponge painting, except for the different kind of arm movement required. Acquire the type of paint rollers commonly used for finishing work in house painting. These are available in different shapes, sizes, widths, and textures. Rollers made for edging are very narrow. The rollers can be used as is, or they can be modified in the following ways:

- Cover them with various textured materials such as netting, mesh, velvet, dotted swiss, hopsacking, or corduroy.
- Place two or three strips of differently textured materials around one roller. These materials can be glued on, or they can be fastened with Velcro so that they can be changed from time to time.
- Rubber bands of different widths, heavy string, and thick

yarn are other materials that you can wrap around rollers to create unique patterns.

Materials
Three or four rollers

A separate container for each roller, such as a small cake pan, a shoe box lid, or a styrofoam or clear plastic (grooved bottom) meat tray

Paint in colors that will overlap harmoniously

Procedure
Spread a thin layer of paint in each container, and allow the children to experiment with the various rollers. Use a different color of paint for each roller.

Variations
• Use very long, narrow sheets of paper, such as 8" x 24", 12" x 30", or 18" x 40", to encourage arm movement.
• Use light, bright colors with dark paper, and vice versa.
• Use rollers in combination with sponge painting.
• Place a piece of chicken wire over the paper before painting.
• Use musical accompaniment for the movement of the rollers.

Results
In experimenting with the use of rollers, children may
1. *increase their awareness of textural qualities,*
2. *improve motor skills as they manipulate the rollers,*
3. *enhance their rhythmic awareness as they move the rollers back and forth to the rhythm of their own body, with or without musical accompaniment,*
4. *develop concepts of spatial relationships,*
5. *develop concepts of time as they realize how quickly the rollers can cover large areas with paint, and*
6. *heighten their concept of cause and effect.*

PAINTING WITH ROLL-ON DEODORANT BOTTLES

These are similar to paint rollers but much smaller. Be sure that the bottles you use are totally empty of deodorant before dipping them in paint.

Materials

Two or three deodorant bottles
A small dish of thick tempera paint for each bottle
Small sheets of paper

Procedure

Allow the children to experiment with the roll-on bottles.

Variations

• Use dark colors on light paper, and light colors on dark paper.
• Use roll-on bottles in conjunction with paint rollers.
• Use roll-on bottles in conjunction with fingerpainting.

Results

When using roll-on bottles for applying paint, children have an opportunity to

1. *internalize comparisons between rolling with large paint rollers and rolling with the small bottles, each of which calls for a different type of arm movement and control, and each of which covers a given space in a different amount of time and*
2. *expand their use of creative instincts as they explore ways to make impressions with the hard surface of the roll-on tip.*

MORE PAINTING TOOLS AND TECHNIQUES

On the following pages, you will find a variety of activities that use

- eyedroppers (pp. 200–203 and 211),
- squeeze bottles (p. 202 and 210–211),
- straws (p. 210),
- string and yarn (pp. 203–207),
- paper towels, coffee filters, or facial tissue (pp. 211–212),
- toy-car wheels (pp. 207–208), and
- dishwashing pompoms (pp. 207–208).

Whatever tool you use, the paint should be of a consistency that will work well with the particular tool.

You need to experiment yourself with each new tool before presenting it to the children. If the tool is too hard to work with, don't use it. Try something else. If children can't hold it with ease, don't use it. Creative art shouldn't be a burden.

The use of different types of painting tools is valuable because of the involvement of the small muscles of arms, hands, and fingers as children experiment with a wide variety of manipulative skills. With each new tool, a new motor pattern is established. Interweaving one pattern with another increases the children's overall motor skills. Additionally, each new painting tool or technique expands the horizons of the imagination and intensifies the internalization of scientific exploration.

BUTTERFLY BLOTS

These are more commonly known as inkblot pictures, but children love the word *butterflies*. This is an excellent activity for large groups, parties, short sessions, rainy days, transition periods, and those occasions when you want the children to produce something to take home but you don't have much time

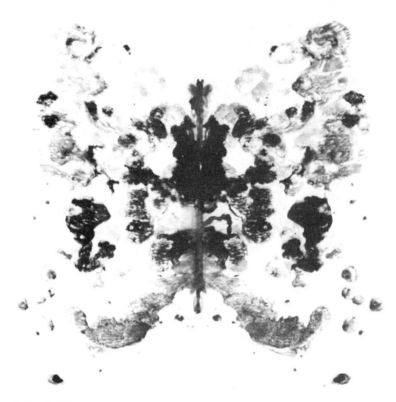

A Butterfly Blot.

or space for the setup or the activity. When mounted on a contrasting paper, a butterfly blot picture makes an excellent gift or greeting card.

Materials

Very small containers (2- or 3-oz.) for the paint, such as the tops of hair spray or shaving cream cans or paper cups

An eyedropper (or medicine dropper) for each container

Paint mixed to a lightly creamy consistency *(the paint should flow through the eyedropper but not be too watery)*

Paper, approximately 6" x 9" or 9" x 12"

Procedure

Each child folds a piece of paper in half, with your help if it is needed. *The paper should be folded precisely.* One introductory method is for you to lightly fold many sheets of paper at once, not creasing them, and then give one piece to each of the children. They may then crease along the fold that has already been suggested. Show them how to match the edges and the corners.

One color is picked up with the eyedropper and squeezed onto one half of the paper in random blots.

The half of the paper without the paint is then folded over onto the half with the paint on it and patted with the hand.

The paper is then opened, and another color is squeezed out on the same half where the first color was squeezed. Repeat the process of folding and patting.

Let each child add as many colors as he or she wants to use.

Hints: Too many colors will cause the design to lose its effectiveness. Adding drops of white at the end helps to set off the contrast of the other colors.

Variations
- Use only primary colors on white paper.
- Use only two psychedelic colors on white, tan, or black paper.
- Use one or two drops of black on a completed picture.
- Use pastel colors only on pastel paper.
- Use pastel colors on black paper.
- Use only black on white paper, or only white on black paper.
- Use related colors (from "Color Wheel," p. 60) for both paint and paper.
- Use related colors of paint on white paper.
- Use seasonal colors according to "Color Guide Through the Year" on pages 58–61.
- Use very thin paint on slick-surfaced paper.
- Rub the hand over the fold instead of patting it.
- Use rough-textured paper.
- Add all colors before folding the paper.
- Use empty mustard squeeze bottles to drop the paint onto the paper.

- For *Large Butterfly Blots,* proceed as above, but use 12" x 18" paper. Mix larger quantities of paint, and drop the paint from brushes (watercolor-type brushes work best). Avoid touching the brush to paper.

Results
This intriguing project helps children to
1. *learn to fold paper as they match edges and corners and then run their hand over the fold to crease it,*
2. *increase their eye-hand coordination skills as they match the corners and edges of the paper while folding,*
3. *develop the control of the tiny muscles in their fingertips as they squeeze the eyedroppers to pick up the paint and then to squeeze it out,*
4. *increase their control of the small muscles of the hand and wrist as they use a brush to drop blots onto the paper when using larger sheets of paper,*
5. *improve their understanding of how to follow a sequence of steps to accomplish a task and to make a design,*
6. *enhance their awareness of cause and effect when they realize that folding the paper makes the image come out on the blank half,*
7. *gain an understanding of symmetry as they realize that one side is the exact mirror image of the other,*
8. *enhance their awareness of color mixtures, color relationships, and color patterns,*
9. *renew their aesthetic appreciation of the finished product, and*
10. *appreciate the feeling of anticipation as they carefully unfold the paper to view the results.*

BLURRED FOLDS

This project is similar to *Butterfly Blots,* and it is also good to use for short or special sessions. A symmetrical design is created in this project by pulling painted string between two pieces of paper.

Materials
  Creamy tempera paint
  Paper no larger then 12" x 18"
  12" lengths of string

Procedure
The children fold their papers lengthwise, as they learned to do for the *Butterfly Blots*.

They each dip a piece of string into a color of paint. They place the string onto one half of the folded paper.

The other half of the paper is folded over onto the half with the string on it.

Holding the paper closed with one hand, each child slowly pulls the string through the folded paper and out. The result is a symmetrical design formed by the string smearing the paint on both sides of the paper equally.

The paper is opened, and then another string with paint on it is placed down on the paper, and the process is repeated.

Variations
• Yarn can be substituted for the string. Thick yarn has a much different effect than thin string.
• Ribbon can be substituted for the string.
• Use three related colors—such as red, red orange, and orange, or blue, blue green, and green—to achieve subtle variations as one string blends the paint into the pattern made by another.
• Use a thin string to apply one color and a piece of thick yarn to apply another.
• Use string and yarn at the same time for another effect.
• Use two primary colors in order to form a third color as they are blended together.

Ben, David, and Todd (all 4½) are making string paintings. This activity is set up in a way that permits children to pursue it completely on their own terms without teacher direction.

- Achieve different effects by experimenting with thin strips of wood or cloth, a piece of lace, a green twig, a weed, or other items that you or the children think of.

Results

This project, which creates blurred designs, will help children to

    1. heighten their awareness of cause and effect,

    2. increase their knowledge of elements of design and color blends

    3. internalize the concepts of mirror image and symmetry,

    4. understand the meaning of blurred, *and*

    5. improve their ability to follow a precise sequence of three steps to accomplish a task.

STRING PAINTINGS

Here again string is used, but in a different way. This is a good follow-up to the *Blurred Folds* activity because it also encourages experimentation.

Materials

> A variety of strings, ribbons, and yarns of different sizes, lengths, and textures
>
> Several colors of tempera paint mixed with equal parts of liquid starch, to help the string adhere to the paper
>
> Containers large enough to dip the string or other material into

Procedure

Children handle this project in two different ways.

One way is to dip the string into the paint and then drag it across the paper to create various designs. Then the string is discarded. The process is repeated with other strings and different colors of paint. Thus, the string (or other material) is used as a painting tool.

The other way is to hold the string vertically over the paper and gradually let it down onto the paper in a particular shape or a free-form design. One child might try to control the way the string is falling to create a specific effect; another might just let the string fall as it will to create its own design. Either way, the string or other material is allowed to dry on the paper. The starch will cause it to adhere, thus making a three-dimensional shape.

Variation

• Mix white glue instead of starch into the paint, and do the entire project on a much smaller scale. Paper should be closer to 9" x 12" in size, and the string or other material much shorter. This will lessen the problems encountered with the sticky glue.

Results

By exploring this activity, children will
1. *extend their knowledge of the physical world through their own experimentation,*
2. *discover that there can be beauty, and even balance, in free-form and accidental designs,*
3. *appreciate the beauty that can be created with common household materials, and*
4. *improve their small motor skills as they work with care in allowing the string to drop onto the paper.*

FREEWHEELING COLOR

The wheels on the small metal cars that children like to roll around make excellent paint rollers. The following is an excellent example of an art project that will motivate children to use materials in a certain way with certain results but without too much verbalization and without patterns to follow.

The painting mounted on a contrasting backing makes an excellent gift.

Materials

Two or three small cars that roll easily

A pan or box lid

A paint pad made of two folded paper towels and placed in the bottom of the pan or lid

Green paint poured over the paint pad

Long, narrow strips of paper, approximately 4"–6" wide and 20" long

A dishwashing pompom (made with sponge strips)

A small, shallow container with a very small amount of a thick mixture of yellow, pink, red, blue, or violet paint (two or more of these colors may be provided)

Black paper, 7" x 24", for mounting the completed painting

Procedure

Allow the children to roll the cars back and forth over the green paint, and then to roll them back and forth on the long strips of paper, leaving green wheel tracks as they go along.

After they have covered much of their paper with wheel tracks, remove the cars and the container of green paint.

Give them the dishwashing pompoms and the dish (or dishes) of yellow, pink, red, blue, or violet paint. Suggest that they press lightly with the sponges so as not to mess up the car tracks. The sparse amounts of color applied with the sponge over the green marks made by the wheels give the effect of a floral scene. Mount the resulting paintings on black paper.

Caution: In keeping with the philosophy of the developmental creative art program presented in this book, avoid telling the child that this is a floral picture. First, each child will handle the material differently no matter how you have structured it. Second, each child will interpret the painting according to his or her own unique perceptions and experiences.

Variations

- In place of the dishwashing pompom, use small pieces of sponge clipped onto a clothespin to make "flowers" over the green paint, or cut the sponge into floral or other shapes.
- Use black paper with green paint; dot with white "flowers," and mount the painting on white paper.
- Try other color combinations.
- Use several shades of green for the paint on the car wheels.

Results

In making these freewheeling color pictures, children will
   1. *grow in self-esteem in response to positive feedback from adults who react to the floral sense of the paintings and*
   2. *use varied muscular control as they change from a rolling motion for the car wheels to an up-and-down motion to print with the sponges.*

RUNNING COLOR

Materials

Paint that has been thinned to a runny, slow-moving, but not watery, consistency

Paper, approximately 9" x 12" or 12" x 15"—small enough so that children can hold it easily

Full-bristle brushes

Procedure

Drop one color of paint onto the paper. Then pick up the paper with two hands and tilt it in all directions in order to guide the flow of the paint.

Repeat the process with another color. Continue until each color provided has been used.

Variations

• Drop several colors at once before tilting the paper.
• Use colors that blend well with each other.
• Use contrasting colors.
• Use several colors, pure or pastel. When the painting is dry, add a few drops of black here and there and tilt. This will provide a dramatic effect and emphasize the colors.

Results

As children tilt the paper from side to side, they will

1. *internalize their concept of gravity,*
2. *become aware of how their own movements can control a process,*
3. *develop control of the hand and wrist muscles as they monitor the degree to which they tilt the paper, and*
4. *enhance their awareness of time because some colors will move over the paper faster than others due to the degree of thinning.*

BLOWING COLOR

This project is the same as *Running Color* except the paint is moved around on the paper by blowing it through straws rather than tilting the paper.

Materials
> Paint thinned out a little more than for *Running Color*
> Drinking straws (wide straws work best; cut the straws in half for the youngest children)

Procedure
Drop the paint on the paper. Blow it around through a straw.

Variations
• Combine the straw-blowing with tilting.
• Use this process with watercolors.
• Use this process on top of completed brush paintings.

Results
In blowing the paint with straws, children will increase their understanding of air movement as they realize they can control it to force paint into interesting designs.

SQUEEZING COLOR

Materials
> Squeeze bottles (such as empty mustard or small catsup squeeze bottles or paint containers with squeeze-top lids)
> Paint that is fairly creamy but thin enough to squeeze out easily
> Paper of any desired size

Procedure
Squeeze the paint onto the paper. Create patterns and designs

by moving the paint container around over the paper during the process of squeezing.

Variations
- Provide circular paper. Squeeze the paint as though decorating a cake.
- Make a cardboard cake shape. Paint it white. Have the birthday child decorate the cake for his or her birthday celebration. This cake can be repainted white after each party. Or you can make a new cake for each child's birthday.
- Decorate containers as gifts. Add milk to the paint (see p. 122) so that the item can be handled without the paint rubbing off too easily.
- Use eyedroppers instead of squeeze bottles for the paint.

Results
This squeezing project will help children to
   1. develop important control of the smallest finger muscles,
   2. realize the possibilities in creating one's own designs, and
   3. enhance the self-esteem that comes with accomplishment.

DIPPING COLOR
This project produces symmetrical designs with the intermingling of colors.

Materials
   Paper towels, coffee filters, or facial tissues
   Thin paint in shallow containers

Procedure
Fold the towel, filter, or tissue into four parts.
   Dip each corner into a container of paint, holding it there just long enough for the paint to be absorbed by the paper.
   Carefully unfold the paper and allow it to dry.

Variations
• Cut small holes in each corner of the towel, filter, or tissue before dipping it. This provides an easy beginning project for the cutting of folded paper.
• Substitute food coloring for the paint.
• Dip each corner into one of four colors of food coloring. When dry, the colors will all have spread out to create a colorful design.
• Dip two diagonal corners into a combination of two colors of food coloring and the other two diagonal corners into a combination of two other colors.
• Dip two diagonal corners into food coloring and the other two into thin paint.

Results
This experimental type of activity helps children to
    1. develop patience and appreciate anticipation as they wait to see what the outcome of their efforts will be,
    2. internalize the concept of absorbency, and
    3. increase their aesthetic appreciation of symmetry.

Pastes

It's fun to smear paste all over the paper. I'm picking it up just like I saw the teacher doing it. Except she put it on little pieces first. I don't want to bother. I'd rather just put it on my big piece of paper. That gives me more room to smear it around. I wonder why she's making her eyebrows go so funny. She looks like she doesn't like what I'm doing. Yesterday she wanted me to smear black fingerpaint all over the paper. This paste hardly even shows. What's wrong with smearing it like I did the fingerpaint? Oh. I see her smiling now. That's good. Now when she tells me not to eat the paste, I'll listen to her. I'll listen because she's learning to let me smear, and that makes me feel good inside. Maybe I'll try sticking on some little circles like she did. Oh, that's the way: Put on some paste, then stick on a piece of paper. Then put on some more paste on top of the little piece and stick another piece on top of that. If I keep doing that, I'll have a great big pile right in the middle of my paper. Pasting is fun.

In pasting activities, your goals may not be the same as those of the children. Even so, your attitude toward whatever they do is important. By allowing them to explore, you enable them to learn the craft of pasting. In the beginning, as they familiarize

In her first experience with paste, Andrianna (2½) pasted scraps of paper on top of each other.

themselves with the material, they must be allowed to get acquainted with it on their own terms. The sensory pleasure derived from smearing is understandable. We realize that the year-old child enjoys squishing and squeezing the breakfast cereal or cooked vegetables around and around in (or out of) the dish. We know that toddlers enjoy playing with sand and mud and water. In giving children paste to experiment with, we are introducing them to yet another material with which they can satisfy their primitive needs to manipulate pliable materials.

While the children are smearing and exploring the paste in their early experiences with this material, they are gradually refining the smaller muscles of their hands and fingers, which will enable them someday to handle intricate pieces of paper that they have cut and to paste them in a deliberate order on a given surface.

Whatever type of paste is used, it should be moist, smooth, and slippery. Fingers are better than brushes for pasting. If you do use brushes, however, be sure they are clean. Do not ever give children brushes that are stuck together with dried-up paste.

KINDS OF PASTE

Library Paste is the best kind for toddlers and beginning preschool children because of its manipulative qualities and especially because it is safe if eaten—a possibility not to be overlooked. Always open the jar before buying it to make sure it has sufficient moisture. If the paste appears to be cracked, try another brand. If you are ordering through a catalog, specify that you do *not* want *dry* paste.

Library paste is available in 5-oz. and 8-oz. plastic jars with spreader tops—plastic applicators that have replaced the brushes that used to come with library paste. It is also available in a 5-oz., easy-to-handle squeeze tube, which is convenient but costs almost twice as much as paste in a jar. Many of today's pastes have a pleasant scent. They can be thinned with water, and they wash off easily from clothing with soap and water.

Wheat Paste is very economical. It comes in a powdered form and mixes easily in warm or cold water. It spreads easily, and, since it is very sticky, it has superior adhesive quality. The extra stickiness can provide an excellent tactile experience for children. Purchase only wheat pastes that are labeled nontoxic and are treated to resist spoilage. **Caution:** Store this paste carefully. It frequently attracts ants.

Cellulose Art Paste is an excellent, very economical paste for paper, cloth, and papier-mâché projects (see p. 268) and for general collage activities. Because it can be easily mixed in cold water by 4- and 5-year-olds, it has developmental sensory implications for children. It is nontoxic and nonstaining.

Flour Paste is paste that you can make yourself or as a classroom project. It is a very satisfactory medium for pasting. It should be carefully made to avoid lumps.

1/2 C. flour
2/3 C. water
1/2 tsp. powdered resin (obtained from a pharmacy)
A few drops of oil of peppermint or oil of wintergreen (as a preservative)

Add the water to the flour a very little at a time, stirring to avoid lumps. Continue stirring the paste until it has a creamy consistency. Add the resin and the preservative. This will make a 1/2 pint of good adhesive paste. In an emergency, flour and water alone can be used as a paste, but it will be rather weak, and it will not last.

Cornstarch Paste is also a good adhesive for children to use, and you can make it yourself or as a class project.

1 1/2 C. water
2 Tb. light Karo syrup
1 tsp. white vinegar
1/2 C. cornstarch
A few drops of oil of wintergreen or oil of peppermint

Mix the syrup and the vinegar together in a saucepan with half the water (3/4 cup). Bring the mixture to a full boil. In a separate container, mix the cornstarch with the remaining water, stirring well until smooth. Add this mixture slowly to the boiled mixture. Stir constantly to avoid lumps. Add the oil. Let the mixture stand overnight before use. The paste will be good for about two months. This recipe will make 1 pint of paste.

OTHER ADHESIVES

Many other adhesives can also be used. In deciding which one to use, remember that all water-soluble pastes and glues usually cause some shrinkage and warping. Paper that has been pasted or painted with these materials will unavoidably curl. This can be prevented, however, by treating the back of the paper with glue, as follows. Turn the paper over so that the back is facing up. Mix 1/4 cup of water with 1 tablespoon of white glue. Use a 2" varnish brush to paint a border around the paper with the glue-water mixture.

Liquid Pastes are not as readily available as cream pastes but are excellent for use on paper since they are treated to prevent much of the usual shrinkage and curling. They must be applied with a brush.

White Glue is sometimes called "plastic glue" since it is made of vinyl plastic. It is an excellent adhesive, creating a strong bond on paper, cloth, leather, lightweight wood, styrofoam, and other lightweight materials. White glue is nontoxic, has no harmful fumes, and will usually wash off clothing after it is dry. It is very white when applied, but it dries clear and colorless. Using white glue teaches children the need for careful manipulation of materials. It is much less free a material than "smearing" paste, and therefore the children must manipulate their materials carefully.

Use the glue directly out of its squeeze dispenser bottle, or thin it with water in a small container for use with a brush over large surfaces. White glue is available in bottles as small as 1 1/4 ounces, which you can refill with glue purchased in larger containers. It is also available in 4-oz., 8-oz., 16-oz. (pint), 32-oz. (quart), and 64-oz. (gallon) sizes. The 4-oz. size is easiest for most preschool children to manipulate.

There are so many brands of this type of glue available that it is a good idea to try out several kinds. Some have better twist-tops than others. Some bottles are easier to squeeze than others, which is a consideration for 2- and 3-year-olds.

Rubber Cement will not cause shrinkage or curling. It is one of the best adhesives to use with paper. Rubber cement is especially good to use when mounting pictures for display because they can be pulled off and remounted if straightening is required. For permanent mounting, the glue can be applied to both surfaces.

The lid must always be put on tightly to prevent the rubber cement from drying out. Keep a supply of rubber cement solvent on hand to thin out the cement, since it has a tendency to dry and thicken. **Caution:** Some children may be very sensitive to the fumes from the solvent. Use the solvent with care, away from the children.

Vegetable Glue is an excellent substitute for paste. It has the adhering qualities of glue, but it can be smeared on with the fingers like paste. Because of its stickiness, vegetable glue presents valuable tactile experiences for children. The can must be kept clean, tightly closed, and stored carefully because it attracts ants.

Liquid Starch, whether commercially prepared or made by you, is an excellent adhesive to use with very thin materials, such as tissue paper, napkins, thin cloth, thread, or thin yarn. It may be applied with a paintbrush. The items that are wet with the starch may dry very stiff to the touch.

Mucilage in a rubber-tipped bottle should be used occasionally to provide yet a different type of gluing experience. It adheres well to paper and cloth, and it dries quickly.

Glue Sticks come in short, crayon-sized containers. The child merely takes the cap off and rubs the semisolid glue (which looks a little like paste) onto the surface to be glued. These are quite inexpensive, but for children, the sticks do not have as much sensorimotor effect as other types of glue and paste.

Roller Glues come in slightly larger containers than the stick glues. The glue is liquid and can be rolled on, similar to roll-on deodorants or rubber-stamp inks.

Fabric Glues are available from craft supply sources. They are especially suited for gluing cloth and other flexible materials.

Tapes are also useful for activities that involve fastening things together. Tapes that you may want to consider using include the following:

- *Masking tape* is best for all-around use for children, because it adheres to so many different surfaces. It should be given to children in a dispenser so that the tape can be torn off with a smooth end. Paper tapes are available in colors (especially around holiday seasons, when they are sold with gift-wrapping supplies), which are interesting to use to make decorative designs.
- *Cellophane tape* is very easy for children to use. Tearing it off of a dispenser is a good exercise for the fingers.
- *Gummed kraft tape* is a brown paper tape that has to be moistened. It is not easy for the young child to handle, but it offers a challenging learning experience.
- *Plastic and cloth tapes* are available in bright colors. They are excellent both for authentic mending chores and for decorative designs.

OTHER FASTENING DEVICES

Accumulate a collection of various fastening devices for the children to use in constructions, collages, arrangements, and other types of art and craft projects. These may include staples, paper clips, paper fasteners, wire, string, and rubber bands.

COLLAGE AND THE ARRANGEMENT OF SPACE

From their first conscious moments, the children have explored the physical space that surrounds them. They have had various kinds of experiences with the physical objects in the environment, such as the playthings with which they have spent much time—on the floor, at tables, in the sandbox, outdoors. From these experiences, the children have been developing concepts about distance, direction, shape, form, texture, weight, and size. They have found that they can fit their toys on certain shelves if they place the toys a certain way. They have discovered that a jigsaw puzzle piece will fit if the shape of the space is the same as the shape of the piece. They have discovered that they need to stand on tiptoe to reach the light switch, and they have learned to fit their feet into the space inside their shoes.

LEARNING THROUGH COLLAGE

Collage making gives children the opportunity to extend these learnings to another dimension. They are able to arrange paper and materials from the environment on a flat surface, such as a piece of cardboard or paper. They have the opportunity to stick things together. They can make a design or arrangement by fastening flat materials to one another or to another surface. They can fasten three-dimensional objects and textured materials to a flat surface.

Collage making gives children the opportunity to explore, to try out, and to discover things to do with the objects and materials they have at hand. Each time the children make a collage, they have the experience of their previous collages to draw from.

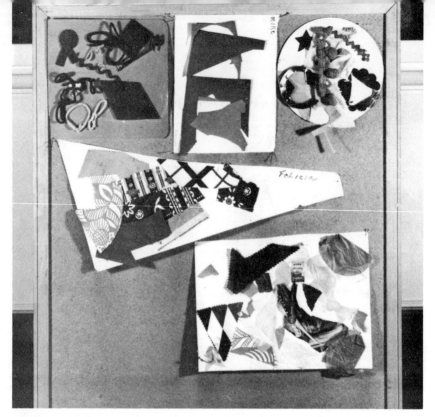

Finished collage projects.

MATERIALS FOR COLLAGES

Collages are made from all kinds of odds and ends, such as interesting pieces of paper, scraps of cloth, plastic, wood, cardboard, old buttons—anything, in fact, that has texture, form, color pliability, plasticity, flatness, thickness, notches, holes, points, eyelets, transparency, or the wonderful, intriguing quality of being absolutely useless—except in a collage.

If you look through your drawers, storage boxes, and wastebaskets, you'll probably find enough items to make any number of collages. But don't stop there. Also check your cupboards, your sewing corner, and your repair supplies. Check out the garage, the attic, the cellar. Clean out old toy boxes, and save old gift wrappings and greeting cards. Ask for a chance to look through the discards from shops, factories, offices, and stores. Even one day's search will uncover a wealth of material from which you can select exciting materials for collage and constructions, or three-dimensional collages.

When you are outdoors—in your own backyard; at the ocean, the park, or a mountain resort; in the country; at the edge of a stream—take a look around and start collecting. You'll find interesting shells and tiny rocks, seeds and pinecones, pine needles and autumn leaves, twigs and straws, interesting pieces of bark, and weeds and dried flowers. If something attracts your attention, pick it up. The uninhibited imagination of children will put all of these things to productive use. For a definitive list of suggested materials, see Appendix A, pages 319–322.

THE USE OF "FOUND" MATERIALS

As the children begin to use "found" materials from the environment—materials that help encourage more direct interaction with the environment—and arrange them in their own ways, they further develop concepts of space, direction, size, and shape. Thus, the children become better able to understand and cope with the physical world. They begin to form their own formulas about where to start, how to proceed, and when to call a project finished. These formulas are internalized; they become part of the organizational and mapping procedures that will be recalled whenever there is a need to plot or map out an area, or to arrange things in that area— whether on a two-dimensional surface or in the three dimensions of actual living and working space.

PAPER COLLAGE

The simplest and most logical starting place for collage work is with paper. To make a paper collage, one piece of paper is applied to another. The opportunities for variety, imaginative combinations, and original ideas are limited only by the paper that is available. The projects listed below are only suggestions from which you can develop your own ideas. These projects can also be combined with projects in other chapters of this book.

PREPARATION

Scraps of construction paper are a good material for beginning collage work. But even scraps need some preparation before they are used.

• Cut the scraps to workable sizes.
• Provide scraps in a variety of colors, shapes, and sizes.
• Store them in some type or order in easy-to-get-into containers to facilitate planning a project for a particular time.
• Keep small containers nearby for ease in taking just as many scraps as you may need for the day, unless the scraps are already stored in such containers.

PRESENTING THE SCRAPS

Present the scraps in an attractive manner. There are a number of ways to do that.
1. Set the scraps on a table in a transparent plastic box (such as a shoe storage box) or in several such boxes from which each child may take materials directly. Other convenient containers are shoe box lids, small, flat wicker baskets, and small disposable aluminum baking pans. I use the disposable aluminum pans often, because their shininess adds to the appearance of great care and concern about the materials—which in turn inspires the children to use the materials with care and concern.

2. Group the scraps on a lazy susan in the center of the working area—either laid out on a large, colorful sheet of paper or in open containers similar to those described in the preceding paragraph.
3. The scraps may be all grouped together, or they may be separated in different containers according to size, shape, or color, or all three. Different ways of separating the materials should be used at different times, because each way presents a different type of eye-hand experience and coordination practice.

For any type of collage, present a limited quantity of materials at one time. Too many pieces of different colors, sizes, and shapes can be as frustrating to children as no variety at all. If there are too many pieces, or too few, the children may just grab the first ones they put their hands on rather than consciously selecting the components of their collage. As a rule of thumb, provide about four or five times as many pieces as each child might use on one collage.

PRESENTING PASTE AND SCISSORS

Provide a small jar of paste for each child or each group of two or three, or use a lid of a cottage cheese carton or some other plastic container with one teaspoon of paste placed in the center. Seashells make intriguing individual paste holders.

Set the paste to the left of each child's place, or put it between the two or three children who are sharing it. Each position calls for a different type of eye-hand coordination, so both methods should be used at different times.

Provide scissors only after the children have had some experience in collage making without scissors.

MAKING A COLLAGE

Once you have prepared the area and provided the materials, the children should be allowed to do as much as they can without adult intervention. If they are new to collage making, you may need to show them how to put the paste on one side of a small piece of paper and press that side down on the larger background sheet. Even after these directions, however, most young children will persist in putting the paste on the background paper and pressing the smaller piece onto it. If they do this, leave them alone. They'll soon figure out through their own experimentation that the other method usually works best.

Variations

There are endless variations of colors, sizes, and shapes of collage materials. By providing contrasts and differences in the paper scraps and cutout shapes, you ensure interest, promote originality, and help children develop a wide range of concepts. Here are some ideas for paper collage.

- Dark background paper with light pieces to paste on, or the reverse—for example, dark blue, dark green, brown, or black background with yellow, orange, and white pieces to paste on; white, yellow, or orange background with only dark colors to paste on.
- Use all related colors—for example, dark blue construction paper background with three shades of lighter blue scraps.
- Use one color for the background and several shades of its opposite to paste on—for example, purple construction paper background with orange, red orange, and yellow orange scraps.
- Use only primary or secondary colors on white or black paper.
- Use a dark construction paper background with long, narrow strips of torn white paper.
- Use a cardboard background with geometrical shapes cut out

David (4) applies scraps of cloth and tissue paper with liquid starch.

of cardboard to paste on. You may need to use white glue for this project, depending on the thickness of the cardboard and the strength of the paste you have been using.

- Use a round-shaped paper background with round shapes of various colors and sizes to paste on.
- Use a round-shaped paper background with round shapes of only one color but different sizes, or round shapes of only one size but different colors.
- Use triangular shapes instead of round ones.
- Use long, narrow pieces of paper, approximately 4" x 12", 16", or 20" long and 3" to 5" wide, so that the children need to decide whether they want two pieces to overlap, and if not, how to prevent that.

- Use seasonal colors as a holiday decoration.
- Using *pennant-shaped* paper as the base of the collage is an excellent perceptual motor exercise. Beginning pennants should be isosceles triangles that are approximately 6" wide and 9" to 12" long. After the children have had some experience with pennants, they can be cut 18" long.
- Provide paper cut into circles or squares of different sizes. To assess children's perceptual-motor and problem-solving skills, present some circles that are as wide as or wider than the paper.

  ☐ **Note:** To cut many circles or squares at one time, use ditto paper. It is much thinner than construction paper, pastes down easily, and comes in an array of lovely pastel shades. Ditto paper is also much less expensive than construction paper.
- For *Negative-Space Collages,* cut out shapes inside the paper scraps—for example, cut out a square, a triangle, or a circle inside a small square, or cut out an oval, a triangle, or a rectangle inside a rectangle. Present both the negative-space scrap and the cutout to be pasted on the background sheet. Some children will paste a similar shape inside the cutout space, some will not paste anything inside, and some will paste a contrasting shape—such as a rectangle inside of a circle.

  You can use only one color of paper for the paste-on scraps. Or you can use contrasting colors of paper, but cut each shape out of a different color. This presents a greater challenge because the children must fit in the pieces not only by shape but also by color.
- Have the children cut their own geometric or free-form shapes for pasting. Younger children will have to cut shapes that you have drawn for them. Older children can use stencils or templates to make their shapes. You can make templates by cutting a geometric shape into plastic coffee can lids. The children then trace the shape that they will cut out with a

scissors. **Caution:** Remember, this is a cutting *experience,* not a test for staying on lines.

• Have the children tear pieces of paper for collage scraps.

Results

Making paper collages helps children to

1. *learn the basic techniques of pasting and gluing,*
2. *learn the basic techniques of cutting and tearing paper,*
3. *experiment with the use of space and become more aware of spatial limitations and of the need for planning and organizing,*
4. *develop an understanding of such concepts as seriation and ordering by size,*
5. *differentiate and classify according to color, texture, size, and shape,*
6. *transfer concepts learned through body movement and through manipulative play to a two-dimensional plane, including* big, little, thick, close together, on top of, next to, underneath, far apart, too big, too long, *and* too wide,
7. *experience the necessity of making choices of shape, size, and color of material,*
8. *expand their capability to make aesthetic judgments,*
9. *internalize feelings for design and balance,*
10. *develop the ability to differentiate between the qualities of different types of paper,*
11. *improve eye-hand coordination and visual-motor perception,*
12. *widen their knowledge of the physical world,*
13. *clarify concepts of time as they learn to wait for paste or glue to dry,*
14. *develop social and sharing skills as they share materials with one another, and*
15. *grow in their feeling of autonomy as they are allowed to develop their own processes and products with the materials provided.*

ONE-COLOR TEXTURE COLLAGE BOOKLET

This fascinating booklet of texture collages, each a different color, is wonderful for a gift. Each week, the children make a collage in a different color.

Materials

☐ **Note:** Each week, the background and scraps should all be shades of the same color.

Paper for background (6" x 9" is a good size)

Ribbons and scraps of different kinds of paper, tape, felt, yarn, and other materials (include a variety of textures; cut the pieces in sizes appropriate to the size of the paper)

Glue

Procedure

Children may choose whatever pieces of paper and other material they wish to use. They glue the items onto the background paper in their own fashion.

Each week they make a collage in one color in the following order: Week 1, *red;* Week 2, *blue;* Week 3, *yellow;* Week 4, *green;* Week 5, *orange,* including yellow orange and red orange.

Children who are 4 and over can also make collages in shades of *purple* or *violet* (this is not a clear color for many 2- and 3-year-olds), *whites, blacks,* and *browns.*

Gather each child's accumulated collages. Punch two holes in the left-hand side of each set. Help each child thread yarn through the holes to tie the sheets together as a booklet.

If you wish, you can add an extra page on top for a cover. Give each child a large label on which you have printed, "My Color Book." The child can paste the label onto the cover of his or her booklet. Children who are able to can write their name under the label. You can do it for those who are not able to do so.

☐ **Note:** These are unusually beautiful collages and make excellent gifts. If you have selected the colors appropriately, no matter how the child pastes the items onto the collage, it looks lovely.

Variation
- Instead of the colored background papers, use pages out of wallpaper books. The wallpaper selected should have only one color with white or black. Use large sheets for individual collages rather than small sheets made into booklets (see photo on p. 251).

Results
In addition to what children learn by doing any kind of collage, these one-color texture collages help children to
1. *expand awareness of color differences,*
2. *increase sensitivity to textures and textural differences, and*
3. *heighten self-esteem, as adults show great interest in the different collages and express their appreciation of the beauty of the color books.*

TRANSPARENT COLLAGES
Materials
  Pieces of white paper or cardboard that are at least 12" x 18"
  Containers of liquid starch
  Soft-bristled paintbrushes or large watercolor brushes
  Colored tissue paper cut into geometric shapes: squares, triangles, ovals, rectangles, circles, pennants, diamonds (paper should be cut small enough for children to use directly or to cut into even smaller pieces)

Procedure
Brush the starch either on the background paper or on the scrap to be pasted down. The children can arrange the scraps on the background in any way they wish to.

Variations
- Use random colors.
- Use related colors.

- Use contrasting colors.
- Use seasonal and holiday colors and shapes.
- Along with the tissue paper, supply scraps of transparent cloth, such as organdy, chiffon, dotted swiss, and organza. You may also supply pieces of threads and yarns and other very lightweight materials.
- *Autumn Leaves.* Cut shades of brown, tan, orange, and yellow tissue paper into the shape of autumn leaves. Supply white or light brown wrapping paper in whatever size you want the collage to be.

  Superimpose the cutout leaves over one another with starch. The result is a wonderful ground base for an autumn mural. Children can also make small autumn pictures for themselves in this manner.
- *Murals* (for 5-year-olds and older). Murals, whether large ones done by a group or small ones done by one child, may be created from specific colors provided for making trees, people, flowers, and other semirepresentational forms.

Results

In doing transparent collages, children
  1. *learn about transparency and overlapping and become aware of combinations of colors that form other colors,*
  2. *further develop control of their arm and hand muscles because tissue paper must be handled delicately to avoid tearing, especially when wet with starch,*
  3. *increase their awareness of textural differences, and*
  4. *expand their knowledge of the physical world.*

3-D COLLAGES (ASSEMBLAGES)

After some experiences with two-dimensional designs, you will want to introduce other materials in the collage activities. Small seashells, pieces of wood, or any of the items listed in Appendix A (pp. 319–322) add an exciting new dimension to collage making—and to your entire creative art program.

Since many of these items will be small, you might want to obtain a collection of small boxes, plastic containers, or even egg cartons in which to divide the selected materials.

☐ **Note:** Sometimes the collage items should be all mixed together because of the different types of eye-hand coordination involved in selecting the pieces.

Materials

Cardboard, paper plates, jar lids, or some other heavy material for the background (sizes may vary from 2 or 3 inches to 2 or 3 feet)

Collage items in individual containers, similar to those recommended for the paper collages

Individual squeeze bottles of white glue, or other types of glue

Procedure

Place the glue on either the background or the object to be fastened down. Press the object in the desired position and hold it for a few seconds to ensure that it sticks.

The first time, suggest one or two objects for the children to start with. Then let them select what they want to finish their project.

Variations

• Make a nature collage, using items found on a nature walk.
• Make a seed collage, mixed with leaves or with grains, such as rice or barley.
• Make a bean collage with lima beans, navy beans, black-eyed peas, and other dried beans.
• Use wood only—toothpicks, tiny sticks, tongue depressors, ice cream sticks, wooden spoons, bark, spools, and so on.
• Use white things only, such as popcorn, cotton, lace, white buttons, eggshells, rice, and tapioca.
• Use soft things only, such as feathers, velvet, cotton, felt, fur, and flannel.

- Use round, flat things only, such as washers, toy or wooden wheels, bottle caps, and jar lids.
- Use dry cereal only, such as Cheerios and Kix.
- Use wires that can be manipulated, such as pipe cleaners.
- Use round things only, such as small beads, spools, and peas. These will require careful handling in gluing, and they must be glued to a fairly heavy solid surface so that the necessary handling doesn't make it bend.

☐ **Note:** In areas serving very low-income groups, it is advisable not to use foods, such as cereal, beans, and pastas, for decorative purposes. Choose items instead from the list of nature and "found" items in Appendixes A and B.

Results

Experiences with three-dimensional collage help children to
1. *increase their awareness of texture, shape, size, weight, balance, and other concepts related to the physical world,*
2. *exercise visual-perceptual skills as they reach and search for additional items to use in the collage,*

Jill, Roger, Samara, Nickie, Marc, and Manuel (all 3) are gluing wooden scraps together. When they have finished, they will paint them with tempera. Compare these assemblages with the constructions shown on page 277.

3. expand their abilities to classify, categorize, and organize according to the challenges provided by the available materials, and

4. grow in self-esteem as they appreciate their own creations.

CARDBOARD BOX CONSTRUCTION OR ASSEMBLAGE

The collage ideas presented so far involve pasting or gluing items to a flat surface. The next step in this type of creative activity is to put together three-dimensional objects to form a construction. Cardboard boxes are ideal for this project and will present limitless possibilities to both you and the children. The children enjoy having their parents gather boxes for the class at home.

Materials

A collection of cardboard boxes of many different types and sizes, such as shoe boxes, tiny jewelry boxes, toothpaste boxes, egg cartons, and boxes from soap, cereal, and other household products

Glue and other fasteners

Procedure

There are two ways to fasten and finish the boxes to form a construction. In the first way, you paint the finished construction. The children fasten together a variety of boxes that they have selected, using strings, rubber bands, tapes, and other fasteners, in addition to glue. Provide small objects from your collage collection with which to further decorate some of the boxes. Then paint the completed construction.

The second approach is to paint the boxes before fastening them together. Scrub the boxes first with steel wool to provide a surface to which the paint will adhere more easily. Scrubbing very waxy boxes with a detergent might help, especially if they are first dipped into hot water. You may have to use cleanser

These containers were glued together and then painted. Ingenuity and individuality are evident in each one.

on some. If so, you must put the cleanser on the scrubbing rag or brush so that the children will not inhale cleanser dust. Adding wheat paste to the paint will also help it to adhere to waxy surfaces. Then fasten the painted boxes together and decorate them as described above.

Variations
- Use cardboard tubes from household paper goods or a combination of tubes and boxes. Or use the tubes with round cereal boxes. (For more ideas about using paper tubes, see the following section, "Paper Tube Construction.")
- Use only very small boxes.
- Use only very large boxes for a group construction that the entire class works on together.

Results

Cardboard constructions or assemblages help children to

1. *relate the balance they have learned about in motor activities to the balance that can be created in the physical world,*
2. *deepen their understanding of shapes and forms,*
3. *internalize concepts and functions of gravity, weight, and counterbalance,*
4. *expand temporal awareness because they must hold one item against the other while waiting for the glue to dry,*
5. *find out about small corners, comparative sizes, and the concepts of* underneath, inside, *and* all around *as they reach over and under and in between to paint the boxes,*
6. *learn to improvise as they reinforce the glue with other fasteners, and*
7. *grow in self-esteem as they view their finished products.*

PAPER TUBE CONSTRUCTION

Materials

Paper tubes from household products (which parents are happy to save and contribute)

Tape, scissors, glue, staplers, and other fastening materials

Paint and other materials for decorating the tubes

Procedure

Children may be allowed to fasten tubes together in whatever form of assemblage they are inspired to do and with whatever type of fastening material they choose.

Expand the project with oatmeal boxes, milk cartons, salt boxes, egg cartons, and other types of cardboard containers.

They can further be decorated with spools, buttons, ribbon, bottle caps, paper cups, toothpicks, and a wide variety of collage items.

They can be painted, covered with tissue and starch collage, or decorated with marking pens. The tubes can be painted and decorated before fastening them together, or the entire assemblage can be painted and decorated. Or the assemblage can be covered with aluminum foil for a shiny sculpture.

Variations

- Toilet tissue tubes can be connected with string run through them and then tied together at each end for a flexible assemblage.
- Holes can be punched at both ends of paper tubes, and they can be fastened together with large paper clips. Yarn can be used by children who are able to tie knots.
- Several tubes can be fastened to create a "marble roll." This can also be used for small cars. Which roll the farthest, the marbles or the cars?
- Many paper tubes can be fastened together with either tape, clips, pipe cleaners, yarn, or other fastening materials to create a "train" that reaches across the room—or the length of a hallway or even, outdoors, the length of a building. Fastening the tubes can be an ongoing project for a period of days, followed by painting the tubes.

Results

The learning that will occur from paper tube sculpture is the same as that for box sculpture (above). However, this project also helps children to

1. *further stimulate their imaginations,*
2. *expand their knowledge of shape and form,*
3. *be creative and inventive,*
4. *explore the concept of flexible constructions,*
5. *experience mathematical concepts of measurement, and*
6. *face new types of problem-solving situations.*

OTHER CONSTRUCTIONS

Any of the 3-D constructions above can be embellished by adding empty food cans and cartons, parts from broken toys, old household and kitchen objects, styrofoam blocks and pieces, wood findings, and other materials you or the children may come up with.

Scissors

Benjie was excited when he saw the scissors. Especially when the teacher said he could pick them up and cut the paper she had given him. At home, his mother never let him use her scissors. He took the scissors in one hand and tried to cut the piece of paper he had in his other hand. But nothing happened. The paper kept sliding out between the scissors— still in one piece. The teacher said, "I'll help you get started." She showed him how to hold his hand with the scissors in one place and to move the paper where he wanted to cut it. Meanwhile, she sang this song:

O-pen, shut them, o-pen, shut them,
O-pen and then shut.
Move the pa-per round and ro-und.
That's the way to cut.

AN EGO-BUILDING EXPERIENCE

Learning to use scissors is one of the important ego-building achievements of early childhood. The children discover that scissors give them instant power to make changes in paper and other materials. Though other cutting tools may be forbidden, here is one that the children can use with full approval.

Cutting *looks* easy. Children readily understand the principle of opening and closing the scissors, and they may spend long periods of time trying to master the technique. Tiny, immature finger muscles are not easily directed to move in the manner necessary to guide and control the opening and closing. As previously stated (p. 6), the ability to control the arm muscles develops from the shoulder downward. Development occurs in the extremities *only* after the other parts of the arm and hand have been developed. While the finger muscles are maturing, the children use and strengthen them, thus gradually increasing their skills.

KINDS OF SCISSORS

Provide the best 5", blunt-nosed scissors your budget will allow. Rubber-covered handles are comfortable for young children.

Left-handed scissors should be made available for children who have left-hand dominance. Once they have learned the skill of cutting and have learned to use the left-handed scissors, the children will gradually (in kindergarten or primary grades) be able to make the switch to regulation-type scissors, the kind they will be using throughout most of their lives.

For older children, 5" clip-point scissors may be supplied. Children in the primary grades may start using pointed scissors, with which they can do more intricate cutting tasks.

For toddlers and 3-year-olds, you can provide 4" or $4^{1}/2$" blunt-nosed scissors. Lightweight safety scissors made of plastic are also available for the youngest children.

SAFETY RULES

Safety rules need to be established at the very beginning of scissors exploration. These rules *must* be impressed on the children over and over again. As in any rule-setting process, the most effective way to discuss the use of the scissors with the children is to allow them to "help" establish the safety list. I recommend the following safety rules.

1. Scissors may be used only at the table or the center where they are provided.
2. Children may walk (never run) with a pair of scissors in hand only if an adult directs them to. The scissors must be clasped with the fist so that the pointed end is in the palm of the hand, with the tip barely showing at the bottom. The hand must be held so that the pointed end of the scissors is toward the ground.
3. When giving the scissors to another person, hold the pointed end toward you with your fist wrapped around it. Hand the scissors to the person with the handles toward him or her.
4. Scissors may never be used to gesture or to point at someone.
5. Scissors are only for cutting paper or other materials that the teacher has provided. They are *never* to be used for cutting clothing, hair, or other children.
6. Scissors must always be replaced carefully in the scissors rack, box, or other container they were taken from.

STORAGE OF SCISSORS

Scissors are worthwhile only if they cut well. To help retain the cutting edge, they should be stored carefully. A scissors rack, in which the pointed end is placed downward, provides good protection for the tool. These racks are fairly inexpensive and can save you money in the long run by extending the life of the scissors. An inexpensive rack can be made by punching holes in the bottom of an egg carton or a gift box.

You may prefer to simply provide a small tray or box with

just enough scissors in it for the number of children who can work at the center at one time. Or if children are sitting at their own places doing a group project, you may just want to pass out a pair of scissors to each child and have the children lay the scissors flat on the working surface until they are ready to use them.

LEARNING TO USE THE SCISSORS

To understand the easiest way to use scissors, pick up your own scissors and notice the way *you* use them. Do you hold the paper still and move your hand around the cutting pattern? If so, your motions are like those of the young child who is learning to cut with scissors. The *easy way* is to hold the cutting hand as still as possible and move the *paper*. The best way to cut out a circle, for example, is to manipulate the scissors but keep your cutting hand in the same place while you move the paper, so that the scissors follow a circular path.

If children are having much difficulty in handling scissors, helping them to learn this method can be useful, although not necessarily easy at first. Young children have difficulty in simultaneously doing something different with each side of the body. Thus, it may take some patience and a great deal of practice to learn the technique. Don't worry about where the scraps fall. Let the children concentrate on cutting. Be honest: tell them it is hard.

To give them practice, bring out stacks of small pieces of scrap paper—especially narrow pieces that can be cut with one snip. Provide magazine pictures that you have already cut around. At first, children may just use these pictures to practice cutting paper in half, but gradually they may become interested in cutting around the shapes of the pictures.

Tracey (3½) and Larry (4) are cutting out circles they traced from a plastic coffee can cover.

CUTTING ACTIVITIES

Materials

An appropriate pair of scissors

Paper that can be cut easily

If the paper is too thin, it will be difficult to manipulate, and it may slip between the blades a great deal. Tissue paper, crepe paper, and cellophane fall into this category.

If the paper is too thick, children may have difficulty exerting sufficient pressure to cut through. Thus, avoid posterboard, heavy cardboard, corrugated cardboard, and similar materials until the children are older.

The easiest materials to use are

poster paper (lightweight construction paper),

fadeless art paper,

butcher paper,
newsprint,
ditto or duplicating paper,
thin styrofoam sheets ($^1/_{16}$" or $^1/_8$" thick),
magazine illustrations,
drinking straws, and
broom straws.
Just a little harder to cut are
construction paper,
tagboard,
$^1/_2$" or $^3/_4$" styrofoam sheets,
wallpaper, and
used greeting cards.
Much harder to cut are
flexible materials such as cloth, ribbons, and leather,
heavy, thick materials of any kind, and
wire and pipe cleaners.

Procedure
Allow for exploratory cutting, helping the children as needed to learn the technique.

Results
Cutting with scissors
1. *further develops the motor skills of the small muscles of the hands and fingers,*
2. *enhances overall eye-hand coordination,*
3. *introduces children to the qualities and properties of various types of paper, internalizing awareness of textures and tensile strength, and*
4. *brings about an awareness of quantities and division as they discover a large scrap can be divided into two or more pieces, and that those pieces can be still further divided.*

WHERE TO OBTAIN FREE MATERIALS

Many free paper and other materials can be used for art activities such as cutting. Refer to Appendix B (pp. 323–327) for suggestions. An especially good source is a local printer who is willing to save the end cuts of paper for you.

When you or the children are cutting, save *all* scraps. Store them according to color. They provide good starting points for many collage and cutting experiences.

CUTTING ON LINES AND RECOGNIZING SHAPES

Being able to cut along a line requires the ability to control the individual parts of *both* hands while coordinating the movements visually. I don't feel that cutting on lines is important for a beginner, but recognizing shapes is. If children learn to cut around the general shape formed by lines drawn on paper, they have acquired one of the important skills that should be developed at the preschool level.

Between 4 and 4¹/₂ years of age, most children have matured sufficiently to be able to cut along lines without experiencing frustration and failure. Six-year-olds who are unable to do so may also have difficulty in reading or writing, or both. They should be given a perceptual-motor and visual screening to find the extent of their problem.

TEARING PAPER

Children who are tense will have difficulty learning to cut. I like to give them paper to tear into scraps before they begin to learn how to cut with scissors. Tearing paper is a good exercise for the release of tension, and it helps children to be more relaxed when they finally handle scissors. And even after they have learned to cut, they should still be encouraged to do projects that involve tearing. Interesting collages can result from combining the two techniques.

TORN PAPER COLLAGE

Materials
Thin paper such as tissue paper, newsprint, or paper towels
Library paste
Background paper

Procedure
Torn paper scraps are pasted onto a background paper to make a collage.

Results
Learning to tear the paper into small pieces and use it in a collage helps children to
1. exercise the small muscles of the hands and fingers,
2. release tension and to be relaxed while handling paper,
3. relieve aggressive feelings,
4. develop visual-motor perception,
5. build mechanical skills,
6. gain a sense of accomplishment and self-esteem,
7. enlarge their means for creative expression, and
8. internalize ideas of proportion.

MONTAGE

This excellent activity lets children utilize their cutting, pasting, and collage-making skills to create a picture. A montage is made by superimposing many pictures and parts of pictures on a background to create an overall pictorial design. Usually the montage covers the entire paper, with each picture or part of a picture overlapping so that the background doesn't show. Sometimes, however, a border is left to serve as a frame for the montage.

Materials

Magazines with many illustrations, or pages you have torn out of the magazines in advance (loose sheets of paper are easier for children than magazines they have to thumb through, but both can be provided)

Fairly stiff paper or sheets of cardboard for the background

Library paste or liquid paste

The teacher discusses *happy* feelings with Kira and Georgia (both 5) and Jill and Lori (both 5½) in preparation for making a Mood Collage.

The finished Happy Mood Collages. (Top: Kira's and Georgia's; bottom: Jill's and Lori's.)

Variations

Montage projects are especially good to use in encouraging children to become further aware of their changing moods and feelings, an essential goal of creative developmental art.

• *Quiet Montage.* Look through the pages of magazines with children and let them pick out what they decide are "quiet" pictures. Also ask them to bring quiet pictures from home. They may select things like pumpkin pie, a man's pipe, a mountain top, a bed, a sad monkey, or a set of books.

Provide a blue sheet of posterboard or other mounting materials and library paste.

Each child cuts out his or her own picture and selects the spot to paste it on. Some blank spaces are left, because, as one child observed, "The paper is quiet."

The entire sheet is covered with blue cellophane. That makes the picture really "quiet."

- A *Smile Montage* can be created by cutting out pictures of faces with smiles on them. These can be pasted next to each other, with many of them overlapping, all around a small mirror. When children look at the montage, it reminds them to smile.
- A *Clothing Montage* can help children distinguish between cold weather clothes and hot weather clothes, or among school clothes, play clothes, and dress-up clothes.
- Individual *Happy Montages*. In addition to the group montages described above, mood collages are excellent projects for children to do on their own. The children can select some collage items to add to their montage pictures if they wish. They will tell you what materials represent *happy* to them.
- Make montage-collage pictures of other moods.
- An interesting project is to have children tear the paper into as tiny pieces as they can. This provides excellent finger-tip exercise.

Results

Children usually select pictures for montages purely by subject matter, showing little preference for either color or black and white. Thus, montage projects help children to

1. *experience a mature step toward cognitive growth where logic, rather than color or shape, will be the deciding factor of interpretation,*
2. *further internalize understandings of classification, sorting, arranging, and the division of space,*
3. *find out that art is not only the arrangement of space, but can also be the rearrangement of someone else's pictures,*
4. *enjoy the experience of cooperative planning,*
5. *realize they can make a real contribution to the classroom environment, because the montages are used for reference in the classroom time and time again, and*
6. *build their self-esteem as their montages are loaned to other classes to experience.*

Manipulative
Materials

Poke it and punch it. Then roll it round and round. Twist.
Squeeze. Squeeze it hard. Squash it, flatten it out. Pile it up.
Little tiny pieces, one giant shape. Young fingers and
growing sensitivities explore the very essence of shape. Form.
How to mold a world. How to build the future.

CLAY

Clay is plastic and pliable, mobile and malleable. It is direct
and responsive to the needs of young children and their
emotions. When clay and children interact, there is a rhythmic
flow of kinesthetic sensations that can provide escape for pent-
up energies and satisfy children's needs to express their feelings. The soothing effect of manipulating this tactile medium
can help to unburden anxieties and fears. As tensions are
relaxed, the experience becomes one of intense sociability; it
becomes the time for conversation and the expression of
thoughts. Thus, clay manipulation is an important developmental activity in many ways.

There are several kinds of clay. Use all of them, but not at the
same time. Whatever kind of clay you use, you'll want to set
some simple rules for its use. First, children should know that

clay must be kept off of floors and other people, and that they may not put it in their mouths. Second, they must share.

PLASTICINE

One of the best kinds of clay for beginners is plasticine. Because it contains oil instead of water, plasticine remains pliable and can be used over and over again. It is smooth and does not stick to the hands and fingers, unless it is very warm. It is readily accepted by young children who may hesitate to use the messier pottery clay. The children stacking balls of clay in the photograph on page 253 are all 2¹/₂ years old.

Plasticine comes in varying degrees of softness. Since plasticine can be used over and over, it is best in the long run to purchase more expensive brands. It is usually obtainable through art supply stores. Excellent plasticine, medium-soft in consistency, may be obtained in two-pound bricks. *Buy only those brands whose colors do not come off on the hands.*

Many colors are available. If you want to keep more than one color on hand, select two that will blend well together, such as yellow and green or brown and orange. If you give children more than one color at a time, be prepared to have the colors permanently mixed together.

New plasticine should be rolled into balls about the size of a child's fist before it is used. It should also be rolled into balls before it is put away after each use.

Plasticine does not need to be stored in covered containers and can be kept on open shelves. It will become somewhat firm when not in use, but it is quickly softened by the warmth of the hands or by a few minutes in the sunshine.

No tools are needed other than hands and fingers. Children should not be encouraged to employ sticks and other pointed objects in modeling the clay. These detract from the developmental benefits of finger manipulation.

MODELING WITH PLASTICINE

Materials

Boards for each child's plasticine (Masonite squares make good boards), or plastic table mats or oilcloth placed on the worktable

Plasticine

Procedure

Place a ball of plasticine at each child's place, or leave it in a container in the center of the table and let the children help themselves.

Let them do what they want with the plasticine. Avoid the temptation of providing patterns and models. Let each child discover what to do with it.

MOIST MODELING CLAY

You should also provide moist modeling clay for the children to use. This is traditional pottery clay, and it is available ready mixed or powdered. It is an evenly textured, moist material that can be fired.

Give the children plenty of time to accustom themselves to the difference between this clay and plasticine. Moist modeling clay will stick to their hands and clothing, but it dries quickly and can be brushed off when dry. It is less elastic than plasticine, but it is more responsive to shaping. This kind of clay hardens between uses, and children may be alarmed the first time they see this happening. An explanation of how moist modeling clay differs from plasticine will help them deal with this new kind of clay.

Care of Clay

Modeling clay will be difficult to use if it is allowed to become too dry. If the clay is too wet, however, it may become moldy or

Chris, Steve, Steven, Patricia, Shari, and Nickolas (all 4) share the experience of working with red modeling clay (which is moister than the gray clay shown in the photograph on the first page of this chapter). Using plenty of water enhances the kinesthetic and tactile values of this experience.

even rancid if it is kept too long in a covered container. If you control the moisture properly, however, moist clay can be stored indefinitely.

If the clay is stored in plastic bags, use two of them so that if one gets torn, the other will keep the clay from drying out. I usually dip the bag in water and shake off the excess gently. This provides just enough moisture to keep the clay pliable. After placing the clay in the bag, pat the bag firmly around the clay. For further protection, place the whole thing in a zippered plastic pillow case. Fold over the top of the pillow case and seal it tightly with a rubber band, twist-tie, or clothespin.

Store the clay in a cool place. Any covered box, cupboard, or other container will do. The best container, of course, is a crock especially made for this purpose. For class use, try galvanized garbage cans, which are available in small, easy-to-handle sizes. Moisture can be controlled by putting one or more wet sponges into the storage container.

Another method of controlling moisture is to poke a small hole in each ball of clay and fill it with water before storage.

If you want to store clay for brief periods only—during class time or overnight, for example—just cover it with wet rags or towels.

To test clay that has not been used for a while, roll a small piece in your hands. If it is very sticky, it is too wet. If it cracks quickly, it is too dry.

If the clay has become too wet, spread it out to dry. Brief exposure to the air will soon make it more usable. Spreading the clay on an absorbent surface, such as Celotex or cloth-covered boards, will speed the drying process. After the clay has dried sufficiently, knead it *well* to remove all air bubbles and to smooth it out.

If the clay has become too dry, break it up—smash it if necessary—and soak it in water for one or two days. After the clay has softened, pour off the surplus water, and then treat it as you would clay that has become too wet. Soon it can be made workable again. Don't hesitate to use very old clay. It keeps almost indefinitely.

Each time you reuse a piece of clay, be sure to "wedge" it to remove *all* air bubbles. Clay is wedged by slamming and slapping it over and over against a hard tabletop or clay board. The children will take great delight in helping to do this.

Powdered Pottery Clay

Pottery clay is also available in powdered form at a great saving in cost. Directions for mixing are found on the containers. The experience of mixing the powder helps children understand and appreciate the composition of clay and its uses. The powder can be obtained in an easy-to-mix form in its own plastic bag. Just add water to the bag, knead the clay inside the bag, and it is ready to use.

It is best to mix the clay about two days before it is to be used. Doing so helps the children develop an awareness of time as they anticipate playing with the clay when it is ready.

Color

The color of most pottery clay, whether it is moist or powdered, is buff or gray. Both kinds are also available in luscious brownish orange terra cotta, or "red clay." When dry, red clay is the color of Mexican potteryware and is so strong that it does not have to be fired. Be sure to give the children an opportunity to use red clays. The color increases their appreciation of clays. Because red clay dries more rapidly than the other clays, provide water with which to pat and moisten the clay as the children use it. Show them how to dip their fingers into the water and moisten the clay with their wet fingertips. Some children enjoy wetting and patting the clay to the point where it disappears altogether. When that happens, give them another piece. The process is far more important than preserving the clay. Store red clay as you do buff modeling clay, but provide much more moisture, as it dries out more quickly.

Preparing Clay for Firing

If clay is to be fired, remember that it will dry more slowly on the inside than on the outside. Keep the object covered with wet rags to keep the outside moist until the inside has had some chance to dry. Dry clay shrinks somewhat. Therefore, if the outer layer dries faster than the inside, the object will crack.

If a clay object that is to be fired is larger than your fist, it is a good idea to hollow it out somewhat from the underside to allow for more even drying.

Thin pieces and small pieces dry more evenly than thick or large pieces. Pieces that are too thin, however, will break.

Self-hardening commercial clays that do not need to be fired are also available. They are quite expensive, but good for experimental use on small projects.

Hardening Finished Pieces

If you want to allow the pottery clay pieces to harden permanently, but do not have access to a kiln, add dextrin (obtainable from any drugstore) to the clay before modeling. Dextrin is made from corn and comes in white and yellow. Use only the yellow. Adding 1 part of dextrin to 19 or 20 parts of powdered clay, or 1 teaspoon of dextrin to 1 pound of moist clay will provide sufficient hardening for your use.

If you add dextrin to powdered clay, do so before you mix the powder with water. When using dextrin with moist clay, knead it into the clay thoroughly. Because it hardens clay quickly, do not mix more than you plan to use immediately.

MODELING WITH CLAY

Materials

A ball of clay for each child, the larger the better (and additional clay within easy reach in case they feel that they need more), or put all the clay in one large free-form mass on the table for a group of children to work on together

A plastic cloth spread on the table (instead of individual clay boards because this gives more space for freedom of movement)

Procedure

In the beginning, use pottery clay, whatever the color, the same way you use plasticine. (As with plasticine, avoid patterns and models.) Usually the children need no encouragement to know what to do. They will poke, pound, pull, and pat. They will add more clay to their original pieces and then they will pull them apart. They may form very small individual shapes or pile one big lump on top of another. However the children handle the clay, whatever they make, they will experience the joy of responding to their need for creative expression.

At the conclusion of the activity, roll the clay into balls for storage.

Variation

• *Pinch Figures.* Eventually the children will try to make figures of people or animals. They will usually become frustrated when they try to fasten on arms and legs, a difficult task. Show the children how they can "pinch out" the shape to form the arms and legs. Making pinch figures is very easy for the young child, and it provides an excellent means for further development of the small muscles that control the fingers. If you demonstrate this technique for children, don't put too much emphasis on it and don't leave your own pinch figures intact, so the children won't feel they are models for them to follow.

POT MAKING

Although we generally recommend that you avoid the use of models and patterns, this does not mean that you should avoid all demonstrations of how to handle craft materials. Pottery clay is an excellent medium for the introduction of beginning craft work.

One of the easiest objects for a child to make is the *Push Bowl.* It is made by rolling a small piece of clay into a ball, and then simply punching a hole in it with thumb or fingers. This is as simple for the young children as any craft can be, yet it contains all the elements of creative productivity.

Introduce Push Bowls only after children have had many months of free-form expression. Again, it is not necessary to provide a pattern. Motivate them by making three or four bowls yourself, while they watch. Talk to them about what you are doing. After each bowl is made, roll up the clay and start another. Also make some free-form bowls, but roll them up each time so that the children will not have a model to copy.

After your demonstration, suggest to the children that they take some clay and find out for themselves how easy it is to make a bowl. Tell them they may make a Push Bowl like you did, or they may improvise. Their bowls may not look like bowls to you, but they will not be merely copies.

Results

Working with clay is one of the most beneficial creative activities for a child. The manipulation of the clay will help children to

1. *greatly improve their control of the small muscles of their hands and fingers,*
2. *internalize the concepts of flexibility and plasticity,*
3. *learn about adaptability and unpredictability, and messiness of clay,*
4. *increase their awareness of three-dimensional shape and design and of the effects of gravity,*
5. *gain experience in problem-solving because of the unpredictability of the clay,*
6. *take responsibility for caring for the materials and practice sharing materials and ideas,*
7. *take pride in their clay pieces as they create new shapes, and*
8. *release tensions as they pat, pound, pull, and tear apart pieces of clay.*

PAINTING CLAY

Red, gray, or buff pottery clay may be painted with tempera when dry or after being fired. Adding canned milk to the tempera will make it semiwaterproof. If the clay is going to be fired, the painting can be done first with "slip colors" obtained from a pottery shop.

Materials

Several bright, clear colors as well as white, which is very attractive on clay pieces (offer the white paint as an accent *after* they have finished with the other colors)

Good-quality watercolor brushes with fine points

PLAY DOUGH

Play dough and other similar homemade materials should not be used in place of clay. They can be used, however, as extensions and reinforcements of that manipulative material.

Provide rolling pins, cookie cutters, modeling tools, and other such accessories for the children to use with play dough if you wish.

Flour, salt, and water are the basic ingredients of play dough. Here is the basic recipe for general use and to make cookies, pies, and other make-believe foods.

> 3 parts flour
> 1 part salt
> 1 part water

Knead the ingredients until they take on the proper consistency. If you vary the proportions, make sure that the amount of water is equal to the amount of salt.

Play dough can be kept in good condition for about two weeks if it is kept in an airtight container. By adding 1 teaspoon of alum for each 2 cups of flour, you can keep the mixture for several months.

Variations

- Add food coloring to the water to color the dough.
- Add salad oil (1 tablespoon to 1 cup of flour) to make the mixture more elastic.
- For modeling small objects to be hardened and later painted, make *Salt Dough,* using more salt and less water than the basic recipe. When a larger amount of salt is used, alum is less important because salt also acts as a preservative.
- For very young children make soft, pliable *Cloud Dough.*

> 1 C. salad oil
> 6 C. flour
> 1 C. water

Jeri (4) and Rael (3½) carefully combine the ingredients for play dough. The quantities of the ingredients placed on the table are controlled so that the children can only experience success, although they may have to experiment with various combinations to achieve the proper consistency.

Use just enough water to bind the mixture. Start with the quantity called for in the recipe and then add 1 tablespoonful at a time if more is needed. Knead the mixture. Cloud Dough will be very oily, but it supplies an unusual tactile experience.

- *Cornstarch Dough* is another interesting kind of dough.

    1 C. cornstarch
    3 C. salt
    1 C. water

Heat the water and salt for a few minutes. Then slowly add the cornstarch, stirring until well mixed. Knead the dough and add more water if necessary. This dough will dry without cracking.

- You may also want to try *Oatmeal Dough.*

    1 C. flour
    2 C. oatmeal
    1 C. water

Add the water gradually to bind the mixture. A couple of tablespoons of cornmeal or one tablespoon of coffee grounds, or both, can be used to vary the texture. Too many grounds, however, will prevent hardening.

DOUGH MAKING

The finest play dough experience that you can give to children is to let them make their own. Almost any combination of the basic ingredients will result in a satisfactory dough. Even if the children do not get around to making anything with their dough, they will have grown in their overall learning by having mixed it.

SUPERVISION

When children perform self-directed experiments, such as making their own play dough or paint, it is usually best to restrict the number of children working in any one area at a time to two or three. A group of this size has the best balance of freedom and self-supervision. They are able to share with one another, give each other assistance, and make suggestions, while still concentrating on their own individual experiments.

If there are more than three in a group, the experience is apt to become teacher-dominated with too many directions. It is always easier to supervise small groups with each individual working on his or her own experiment than to watch over one large group in which everyone is supposed to be doing the same thing. With one large group, too much of your attention may be diverted to the child who is deviating or the child who is setting the best example. The children between these two extremes may be ignored; you will have difficulty in recognizing and meeting their individual needs. This holds true for almost any type of classroom activity.

Materials

Small quantities of ingredients for each group of two or three children

A bowl of flour and a scoop

A smaller bowl of salt

A small scoop for salt (unless you use a box of salt that can be poured)

A small pitcher of water

A dispenser bottle with a very small opening for salad oil (liquid sweetener or hand lotion bottles are satisfactory)

A small container (such as a disposable aluminum foil baking pan or bowl, or a large plastic cereal dish) in which each child can mix his or her own ingredients

Tablespoons for mixing with (the children will soon discard them in favor of fingers and hands, however)

An extra amount of trust

Procedure

If the children seem to be stuck, suggest they experiment to find out if they need additional quantities of one or more of the ingredients. They may try oil, water, and salt before discovering themselves that the mixture needs more flour.

Tell the children that when the mixture does not stick to their hands, it is ready to use.

COLORING THE DOUGH

Extend the children's interest in this important activity by adding small amounts of food coloring or powdered tempera to the dough. Since making play dough is a somewhat complicated procedure for them, it is best to save the addition of color until after the dough is made.

The color can even be added the next day. Then the children can use food coloring with plastic droppers to color their dough.

Or they can sprinkle powdered tempera onto their mixture. Either way, they must knead in the color until it is blended. Most children will make their dough quite oily, and the color will blend in easily. If the mixture is fairly dry, however, it will not take the color as well.

☐ **Note:** When you are mixing dough yourself for the children to play with, you can add the powdered tempera directly to the flour before mixing. This is not a good method for the children, however, because it does not enable them to experience the extra finger manipulation involved in adding the color *after* the dough is mixed.

Some children have much difficulty in manipulating their fingers so as to mix in the color. The observant teacher can use this as a clue to which children may need more experiences in developmental activities for increasing fine motor skills.

Results

When making play dough, children will

1. *increase their knowledge of proportion, quantity, and measurement,*
2. *develop a conceptual awareness of the difference between measuring dry ingredients and liquids,*
3. *expand their awareness of textural differences and sensitivity to touch,*
4. *internalize concepts of oily, floury, sticky, mushy, thick, thin, and other descriptive words,*
5. *experience the emotional well-being that accompanies satisfying sensory explorations,*
6. *display an awareness of their own creativity and inventiveness as they show a strong possessiveness for their own dough, and*
7. *develop their finger muscles, including their fingertips, when they knead the dough and when they add color to the dough.*

PAPIER-MÂCHÉ PULP

Papier-mâché activities should be reserved for children who are at least 5 years old.

Have some children help you tear three double sheets of newspaper into small pieces. Unfold the paper before tearing it.

Completely cover the torn paper with boiling water. Let it stand in the water a few minutes; then stir the mixture until it forms a pulp.

Mix 6 tablespoons of wheat paste with 2 cups of water. Stir this mixture into the wet pulp. When it is cool enough, knead the pulp with your hands until it is well mixed and sticky.

This mixture can be used to shape small objects. After the objects are dry, the children can sand them smooth and paint them.

It is best to mix the pulp just before use. It does not keep for more than a couple of days, and then only if it is stored in a completely airtight container.

There are also many commercial preparations that can be used instead of homemade papier-mâché.

CHAPTER 11

Woodworking

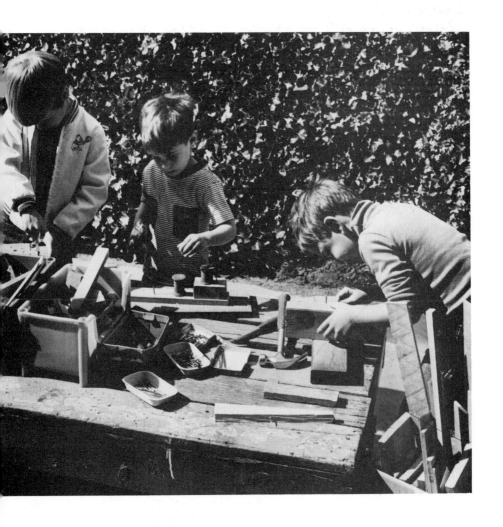

Driving past a new construction project with my 2-year-old grandson, I slowed the car down so that he could see the wonderful things that were going on. But he began to cry: "Poor house. All broken. Man break house. Bad man." He saw people doing all kinds of no-nos. Two years later, he was the proud owner of a man-sized tool chest, complete with small but very real tools of all kinds. A saw. Hammer. Hand drill. Level. Screwdriver. Vise. A tape measure and a T square. And he knew how to saw a piece of soft wood, glue it, hammer it, or even sometimes tape it. He decorated his pieces with all kinds of intriguing items he had picked up around his home: a broken comb, a peanut shell, a piece of tile, a cardboard box. He had a wooden box, around whose four edges slots for sawing had been started for him. This enabled him to work independently. But whether he was sawing, gluing, decorating, or putting everything away, always one thing was overwhelmingly in evidence: pride. The pride of accomplishment that comes with the proper handling of real tools; of building, not tearing down; of creating, not manufacturing.

WOOD IS A LIVING MATERIAL

Woodworking enables children to explore the physical aspects of their environment and gives them an opportunity to create something new of their very own. First, they make a choice, selecting the material they wish to use. Perhaps they know in advance what they want to do with it, or perhaps they just want to "work," exploring the role of an adult. Children like to saw and hammer. The physical activity, the concentration, the release of emotional energy and aggressive feelings—all these things make them feel good. Wood is a living material and children like the feel of it. They like to touch it and even to smell it. With a little guidance, they can learn to take a simple block of wood, sand it smooth, wax it, and buff it. And they can learn about fine craftsmanship.

THE WOOD SUPPLY

White pine, spruce, and poplar are soft woods that children can saw and hammer easily. The wood should be smooth and free of splinters and knots. Boards should be cut with the grain running lengthwise. To check this, lay the board on a flat surface and look at the side. The grain should run horizontally rather than vertically or at an angle.

You can use

balsa wood, which is very soft and easy to use, but is quite expensive,

pine moldings and dowels, and

all kinds of wood scraps, shavings, spools, knobs, wooden buttons, and similar items from a cabinet shop.

The children can practice sawing the edges of wooden crates. Make ¼" slots every 2 inches around the top edge of the crate.

They can use these slots to saw with a minimum amount of supervision.

Outdoors, the children can saw on and pound nails into tree stumps and logs. They can also make use of twigs, branches, roots, and other kinds of wood found outdoors.

Scraps that are not cut with the grain or that have knots should *not* be used for sawing, but may be used for *gluing* activities. Plywood scraps, which are difficult to saw and hammer, are also good for glued constructions. Wood-gluing constructions are an excellent tie-in between block building and carpentry.

You can supplement your wood collection with
wallboard,
pegboard,
cork,
floor tile and other scrap building materials, and
styrofoam blocks, which are especially good for toddlers.

Dani (5¹/₂) at the workbench. The board he is sawing is nailed to the bench with two nails.

Dani's picture of himself at the workbench. The elaborate headdress is an indication of the feelings of importance and satisfaction that resulted from the woodworking experience—feelings that were enhanced by the fact that he was photographed while doing it.

THE WORK AREA

When carpentry tools are used, a work area should be set up away from the flow of classroom traffic and away from other children who are playing. Workbenches should be about 15" from the floor, and they must be sturdy. A suitable workbench can be made from two child-sized sawhorses (or from two adult-sized sawhorses that have had the legs cut down). Place the sawhorses about 3 or 4 feet apart. Then nail a heavy board, at least 2 inches thick, to the two sawhorses. One child can hammer and saw at each end of the board, and use the space between the sawhorses for tools and supplies. Any heavy table that is an appropriate height can also serve as a workbench.

TOOLS

Vise. Children cannot usually get good leverage while they are sawing. Therefore, a vise should be used to hold the wood in place in case the saw slips. If a vise is not available, nail the wood to the workbench to hold it securely in place while the child is working on it. Use two nails to prevent pivoting.

Hammer and Saw. The two basic tools for working with wood are a hammer and a saw. Toy ones are unsatisfactory. Therefore, provide children with small-sized *real* tools. Before buying a hammer, make sure that the head is securely wedged in place. You should also provide children with a claw hammer for pulling out nails. This can be a regular-sized tool. Cross-cut saws that are short and have sturdy handles are the most desirable kind of saw for young children.

Drill. A drill for boring holes in wood is another valuable woodworking tool. A hand drill that works like an old-fashioned eggbeater is easier to manipulate than a brace and bit. Toy electric drills are available, and they work well on soft wood.

Other Tools. The children should also be introduced to other tools at this time, including pliers and screwdrivers. These should be real tools, sturdy and of good weight, but not very large. (**Caution:** A rasp is dangerous for young children, and it should be used only under very close supervision.)
Include the following items in your woodworking supplies:

a 4" screwdriver,
a pair of pliers,
metal squares and rulers,
levels (a toy level, if it really works, is satisfactory), and
a wide variety of screws and nails.

Nails with large heads are preferable, but the children should also have the opportunity to work with 6-penny and 8-penny nails. *Avoid* roofing nails, for they can be quite dangerous if they are stepped on.
Screws that are narrow and have flat heads are easier for children to handle than those with rounded tops.

RULES FOR WOODWORKING ACTIVITIES

For the children's safety, certain rules must be followed when they are working with tools. They should be helped to understand what the rules are and to know why you expect them to obey them. The rules should include the following:

1. Tools must always be handled properly and with care.
2. Tools must never be laid on the workbench when someone is through using them. They must instead always be replaced in the tool box or hung on the appropriate hook.
3. Tools must never be taken away from the immediate working area.
4. One child must never hold a board in place for another. Such boards need to be either nailed to a solid surface or gripped by a vise.

If you have one or more children who are not ready to follow the strict rules that are necessary for safe woodworking activities, it is possible to give them similar experiences that are in the realm of their readiness. For example, you can let them saw on the sides of wooden boxes, using a precut slot for a starting point. You can let them saw on logs or tree stumps out of doors. You can give them very soft wood and a lightweight hammer for pounding nails. You can present scraps of wood with predrilled holes to pound nails into. You can also let them hammer nails in pieces of Celotex or styrofoam.

WOODWORKING ACTIVITIES

Children will find many things to do with wood and tools. They can

- saw, hammer, and drill holes in wood.
- use sandpaper to smooth surfaces, edges, and corners of one piece of wood or of a construction they have created

with two or more pieces of wood nailed or glued together.
* create abstract constructions or representational objects.
* join in a group project to build a construction, which may be just a simple piece of wood with several other pieces nailed on, or it may be as ambitious a project as the frame of a play building.
* attach wheels that turn when given the appropriate fittings (this can be done with just a small block of wood, appropriate to the size of the wheels being used).
* glue wood scraps together to create fascinating sculptures and stabiles (this is a good project for wood pieces obtained from cabinet and furniture-making shops).
* help repair wooden playground equipment and classroom furnishings.

Materials

Wood scraps of all kinds
Appropriate tools for sawing, hammering, drilling
Glue (optional)
Worktable with a vise
Sandpaper
Paint (optional)

Procedure

Allow children to explore and create their own woodworking processes. This activity must have direct supervision by adults at all times, however.

Finishing

When finished with a project, the children may wish to decorate the things they have made with a permanent finish. They can use any of the following:

Powdered tempera paint mixed with milk instead of water
Powdered tempera paint mixed with wheat paste and milk
Water-based acrylic paint
Enamel over a good undercoat

Wood constructions. The two small ones in front and the large one on the right were made by 3½-year-olds. The large one in the center was made by a 4-year-old, and the large one on the left by a 5½-year-old. Both girls and boys enjoy this activity.

Clear shellac or varnish
Clear plastic finishes
Crayons

Results

Children derive a great deal of satisfaction in creating with wood and in using real tools. Among other things, they

1. *develop a sense of power and self-esteem because of using adult tools and doing adult-type projects,*
2. *learn carpentry skills in accordance with their level of ability, including the handling of tools with care,*
3. *develop an awareness of their relationship to others as they learn to handle the tools in a way that will not cause danger to their peers and learn to keep sufficient space between themselves and others,*

4. *experience the process of making a plan and carrying it to a conclusion,*

5. *expand their understanding of the concepts of weight, thickness, shape, volume, length, and width,*

6. *are able to release emotional tensions and satisfy needs to express aggressive feelings in a legitimate manner,*

7. *develop new concepts of representational design as they begin to relate what they make to the real thing, and*

8. *sometimes follow up a satisfying carpentry experience with their first attempts at representational drawings (see photos on pp. 272 and 273).*

WHITTLING

Five-year-olds can be taught simple whittling procedures, but even the most skilled children will require close supervision.

Materials
  Small paring knives
  Small twigs (each child selects a 10- to 14-inch twig from a
    pungent bush or tree)
  Sandpaper squares, approximately 4" x 4"

Procedure
Show the children how to move the paring knife gently along the twig—always away from the body. Review with them the following rules:

1. Always keep your eye on the knife so that you know what it is doing at all times.
2. Whittle slowly and gently.
3. Always whittle away from the body.
4. Support the hand holding the twig by resting it against your body to keep it steady.

    Sit next to the children as they begin whittling. Give them help as needed. Show them how to use sandpaper to smooth the wood when they are through whittling.

Results

In learning to whittle, children

1. *learn to handle a knife appropriately and with extreme caution,*
2. *learn to perform a task according to a given method,*
3. *develop self-esteem as they accomplish so adult a task,*
4. *exercise eye-hand coordination and visual-motor perception, and*
5. *experience heightened kinesthetic awareness as they learn to hold the twig steady by bracing the hand against the body.*

CHAPTER 12

Styrofoam

It was just a piece of styrofoam, cut round to resemble the shape of a birthday cake. The teacher had glued it to a piece of heavy cardboard, also round, but larger, to hold the lightweight material in place while it was being worked on. Today was Anna's birthday and her friends helped her to decorate "the most beautiful cake in the world." It was festooned with green and pink pipe cleaners which sprouted abruptly in surprising but harmonious clumps about the top surface. Around the upper rim of the cake were dozens of pastel-colored toothpicks, around which had been woven in a delightful 5-year-old unpattern, strands of pink and green yarn and ribbons, whose many loose ends casually hung over the edge like scraggly bangs. Here and there various sizes of candles blossomed out of the surface, their tips decorated with bits and pieces of aluminum foil, giving each candle the appearance of having several silver-flamed tops. A few sparkling jewels from the collage collection completed the creation. It was lovingly carried to the table where the birthday party, with cupcakes and bonbons, was about to begin.

Styrofoam and other brands of molded plastic foam are inexpensive, lightweight, easy to handle, interestingly textured, and have an easy-to-poke-into surface that lends itself well to the creative activities of young children. The ease with which it can be controlled makes it highly satisfying to children. The ease with which it can be obtained makes it highly satisfying to teachers, who worry about budgets and sources of materials.

VARIETIES OF STYROFOAM

Styrofoam may be purchased commercially in many different shapes and thicknesses. It can be obtained in sheets so thin that they can be cut with scissors. Larger pieces, up to 4 inches thick and 1 foot wide, are also available. These thicker pieces can be easily cut with an ordinary bread knife or a small saw. (**Hint:** Smooth the cut edges and sides by rubbing this with another piece of styrofoam, as you would rub sandpaper on wood.)

Commercial styrofoam is generally obtainable in white. Blue is also fairly popular, and green styrofoam is frequently used by florists. Styrofoam paint is obtainable in spray cans, but we generally do not use it in nursery school or kindergarten. (If used at all, it is used by adults only, as are other sprays, for safety reasons.)

SOURCES OF STYROFOAM

Scrap styrofoam and plastic foam are readily available. The best places to get them are electrical and electronic supply houses, since much of their equipment comes packed in it. These packing pieces, which may also be obtained from hardware stores, usually come in interesting shapes, since they have been formed to encase the merchandise with its exact shape.

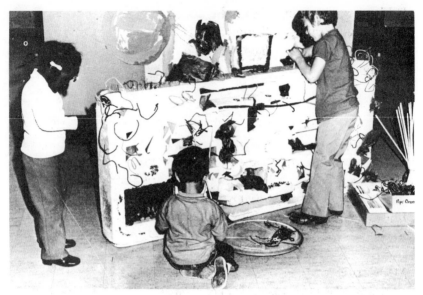

Many children have had a hand in decorating the styrofoam motorcycle packing mold. Saundra (3½) is beautifying the upper left corner with hairpins. Bradley (4½) is trying to find a way to stick on some oversized drinking straws, which bend too easily. Seth (5½) is adding popsicle sticks, which are also difficult to stick into the tightly pressed foam.

People who decorate for banquets and parties also use styrofoam, and they may be willing to give you their leftover scraps. Florist shops, too, frequently have such scraps.

Try to keep on hand large squares and rectangles, balls of various sizes, flat pieces in various shapes and thicknesses, pieces thin enough to cut with scissors, cones and dowels (which are especially available during the Christmas season), scraps cut from larger pieces, and packing shapes and forms.

Some items that are useful in decorating these various types of plastic foam and in making stabiles are

Artificial flowers	Clothespins	Jewelry
Beads	Corks	Macaroni and
Broom straws	Drinking straws	spaghetti
Buttons	Feathers	Nails and screws
Chains	Ice cream sticks	Pipe cleaners

Ribbon, yarn, and other trimming	Thread	Wire strips
	Tongue depressors	Wood dowels
Spools	Toothpicks	Wood scraps
Springs	Twigs	

STABILES

Unlike mobiles, which are delicately balanced forms that hang and sway with the breeze, stabiles are fairly easy for very young children to create without much adult assistance. Stabiles are similar to mobiles except that they do not hang and their parts may or may not move.

Materials

A piece of styrofoam or other plastic foam (you can make several sizes available)

An assortment of collage items (such as toothpicks and other things that children can stick in) with which to decorate the stabile

Procedure

Usually the children will stick on a few items and let their imagination take them from there. Let the children know that they may use the materials in any way they wish to make their own designs.

Variations

- Have two or three children work on one large project. Combine paint, three-dimensional materials, and imagination.
- Have the children glue together very small scraps of styrofoam and then decorate the objects with paint, scraps of cloth, and other appropriate items.
- Limit the children to only a few selected materials, such as round styrofoam balls and pipe cleaners.
- Have the children paint the plastic foam before they decorate it. Use tempera paint on styrofoam, and watercolor on the

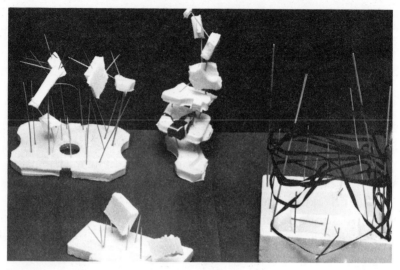

Styrofoam assemblages are usually put together and taken apart many times during an activity session when they are in use. The small piece in front was assembled by a 2½-year-old. The other pieces (from left to right) were made by a 3-year-old, a 4-year-old, and a 5-year-old.

smoother-finished plastic foams. Marking pens are good for decorating with designs.

Results

When making stabiles, children will display amazing ingenuity in the way they combine the materials. They will

1. *experience problems of balance and weight as they decorate one side of the stabile too heavily and learn to solve this difficulty by counterbalancing,*

2. *enter into this activity readily, even if they are hesitant about painting or clay work (stabile making is one way to introduce confused or hesitant children to creative experiences),*

3. *practice many of the manipulative tricks they have learned from the various table games, puzzles, blocks, and similar materials that are part of their daily play, and*

4. *increase their aesthetic awareness as they work to make their pieces beautiful.*

Print Making

*It can be fingerpaint handprints all over a paper tablecloth
to decorate for an open house. It can be circles in neat rows
made from spray-can tops dipped in paint. It can be squares,
triangles, or free-form shapes made from a wide variety of
gadgets, parts of games, or cut into pliable material, such as
vegetables or erasers. However it's made, whatever the
material, it's learning about design.*

Print making is a simple method of transferring a design from
the surface of an object to some other surface, such as a piece
of cardboard or paper. The object is dipped in paint or ink and
then pressed or stamped on the surface onto which the design
is to be transferred.

Print making introduces a new concept to the children: the
reverse image. Except for a few projects, such as *Butterfly Blots*
and *Monoprints* (pp. 200–203 and 181–182), the art experiences we have discussed so far all involve fashioning or creating something directly. Now, with print-making projects, children will discover that the design they make will be reversed
when they print it.

Phyllis (4) prepares a paint pad to use in making white valentine prints on red paper. Her tools include a heart-shaped kitchen sponge, a heart-shaped potato half, and the end of a carrot.

MATERIALS FOR PRINTING BLOCKS

The children can employ a wide variety of articles in making prints. Here are some they can use directly, without having to change in any way:

Bottle caps	Jar lids	Spools
Checkers	Kitchen utensils	Wood blocks
Cookie cutters	Plastic toys	Wood scraps
Dominoes	Seashells	
Erasers	Sponges	

In addition to these materials, you can cut original designs or geometric shapes into art gum or other kinds of soft erasers.

A utility knife works well on art gum.

You can also cut a design into root vegetables, such as carrots, potatoes, or parsnips. You can use a cookie cutter to form the outline of a design in a potato and then cut away the edges. For Valentine's Day, I like to cut valentine shapes out of potatoes and then brush white paint around the edge of a doily to make lacy prints around the hearts.

You can make small, individual printing blocks for each child from plasticine. With a toothpick or some other implement, children can scratch an outline onto the surface of one end of the block themselves.

Another interesting printing device can be made by gluing pieces of felt, cork, cord, and other materials onto the surface of a small paint roller. Dip the roller lightly in paint or ink and roll it across a piece of paper to produce a design.

Wads of wet paper make yet another kind of printing block. Simply wad a piece of wet paper into a ball, dip it in dry paint, and blot it onto another surface.

PAINT AND INK

Paint or ink is ordinarily applied by pressing the printing block onto an ink pad or paint pad, or by dipping it into a shallow dish of paint (such as a cottage cheese carton lid).

The best kind of paint to use for printing projects for young children is liquid tempera.

Paint pads can be made by putting two layers of folded paper towels in a flat dish and pouring a small amount of tempera paint over them. Let the towels stand for a few minutes until they soak up the paint. (Or you can buy ink pads.) Dab the printing block onto the pad lightly and then press it on a piece of paper to transfer the print.

Older children may want to apply the paint to the object with a brush rather than use a paint pad.

PAPER AND COLORS

Any paper suitable for painting is suitable for printing. Novelty papers can be used effectively.

Use light colors on dark paper, or dark colors on light paper.

Variations
- Use several shades of one color on paper of the same color but in a lighter or darker shade. This will give the design the effect of being printed on the paper by machine.
- Use seasonal colors for holiday projects.
- Make printing blocks in the same shape out of several different materials, and use a different color to print each one in order to create an interesting design.

Finished prints. They can be used for gifts or decorations. Children of any age can make them.

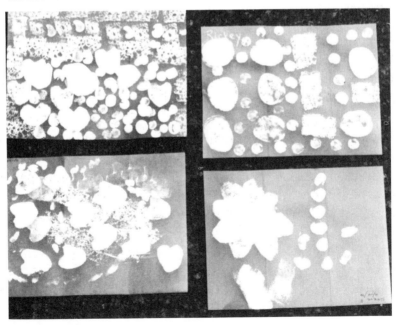

- Print on tissue paper to make gift-wrapping paper.
- Print on muslin squares with ink.
- Print on cardboard rather than on paper.
- Print the design with ink; then paint over it with transparent watercolor.
- Make a design using ink or paints; then finish the project with crayon or marking pen.

Results
When children participate in print making, they
1. *acquire the concept of making reverse prints,*
2. *internalize the concept of mirror image,*
3. *have an opportunity to practice principles of design that they have been developing in their other art experiences,*
4. *enjoy the ease with which they can to create a controlled design and learn the advantage of planning for design,*
5. *increase awareness of space and size as they make a decision regarding what fits into some particular space, and*
6. *develop an awareness of the concept of overlapping, which gives them an introduction to perspective.*

CHAPTER 14

Special Activities

To experiment and to discover for one's own self! To investigate and try out and to proceed at one's own pace! To make one's own selections of materials and to look only within one's own mind to decide their use! The infinite nature of imagination! The thrill of self-discovery! The satisfaction of self-accomplishment! The growth of an individual!

THE ART PARTY

On the morning of the art party there was an acute sense of anticipation in the air. The two teachers with their two assistants felt it. Their thirty-two 4- and 5-year-old students felt it. Perhaps it began when I had suddenly asked them to rearrange their schedules so that the entire group could go out to the playground together at 9:15, shortly after they had arrived. It was a brisk day. The sun was shining, but the air was cold. The movement on the playground was vigorous as the children climbed on, jumped over, and crawled under the equipment. Every wheel toy was in use. The rocking boat had a continuous stream of passengers coming and going. The treehouse platform was resounding with laughter.

The Art Party.

THE CLASSROOM SETUP

When the children returned to their classrooms at 10:15, everything had been made ready. The folding wall between the two adjoining rooms had been pushed back. Half the room was cleared of tables and chairs. Here the children sat down on the floor to have their midmorning snack of juice and crackers.

In the other half of the room, all the tables were crowded together. At each table a different type of art activity had been set up. The children would find clay, collage materials, styrofoam, easels, paint, chalk, crayons, scissors, paste, and a variety of paper.

Through careful planning, a feeling of space had been created—yet the closeness of the tables was deliberate. Here the children could work at their own projects in their own places and yet be closely enough involved with others nearby that the electricity of creative accomplishment and emotional satisfaction would flow from one to another.

One teacher put some lively classical music on the record player, a few balloons were let loose among the children, and they were invited to go across the room and find a place to work.

The orderliness with which the materials had been set out, the casualness of supplementary materials, the placement of the tables and chairs, and the planned predominance of different colors in different areas of the room all made it comfortable and easy for the children to find something to do.

THE ACTIVITY

Everyone became deeply involved in their own activities. From time to time the children would change places. For the most part, the adults found that they were in the way, and they gradually drifted to the other side of the room to become onlookers. Their number gradually increased, for everyone who passed the open doors was drawn into the room by the intensity of feelings that prevailed.

It was the magical hour, one that was strangely contradictory. There was a dramatic tension, but at the same time there was a feeling of relaxation. It was noisy and busy, but also still and quiet. Here was creativity.

The following day, the workshop was repeated. The 3½-year-olds were invited to join the group. To accommodate them, rolls of paper were put down on the floor, together with crayons and chalk. Because of the younger age of some of the children, the working time at any one activity was somewhat shorter. But the same feelings of creative accomplishment prevailed as the children worked side by side. Age differences went unnoticed. Usually restless, aggressive, or hyperactive children were deeply occupied. Throughout the room there was a feeling of complete and mutual involvement.

CLOSING

When the materials were used up and the time for lunch grew near, the record player was turned off and the children were drawn by the rhythmic beat of a tambourine to the cleared area of the room. There they jumped and rolled and bounced. They flew like birds and grew like flowers, then sang enthusiastically in perfect unison:

Are you laughing,
Are you laughing,
Laughing with me?
Laughing with me?
We are all now laughing.
We are all now laughing.
Happily.
Happily.

Gradually, the spell was broken. The children returned to their own classrooms with their teachers. Tables were put back in place and the folding door was closed. Each person who had been involved, children and adults alike, had extended the dimensions of his or her own experience.

Results
In addition to the learning that usually occurs during various creative art activities, the Art Party helps the children to
   1. increase their ability to concentrate and
   2. expand their creative awareness in a general atmosphere of creative industry.

THE ART DANCE

Another type of special art event is the Art Dance. Though similar to the Art Party in that a very large group can participate, the motivations and goals are entirely different. In the Art Party, we have a variety and abundance of materials, working areas that are close together, many children doing the same thing, a constantly changing musical background, limited physical space in which to move, and great earnestness displayed by all.

The Art Dance is characterized by a limited supply of materials restricted in variety, large sizes of paper, spacious working areas, freedom to be close together or far apart, freedom to change activities at any time, a constant repetition of the same musical accompaniment, and a general atmosphere of gaiety and abandon.

ROOM SETUP

The Art Dance came about one day in early spring when doing something special seemed to be in order. Enthusiastically I suggested that the teachers and children all go outdoors to look for the early signs of spring. While they were gone, I cleared the classroom of all furniture except for two small tables pushed against one long wall. Murals the students had painted the day before were put up along the wall behind the tables. Here and there cardboard cutouts of children dancing and jumping set the stage for the coming gaiety. On the tables I placed

a few small cans of tempera paint and brushes,
a few assorted crayons,
some oil pastels and colored chalks,
several percussion instruments from the rhythm band set,
large pieces of paper, some rectangular and some circular,
   scattered in a haphazard manner on the floor,
two long rolls of paper 12" wide, also put down on the floor,
collage materials and glue bottles on two pieces of dark
   construction paper placed in the center of the room, and
   a record player playing softly "Round and Round the
   Village."

The Art Dance.

When the children returned with their teachers, they displayed little surprise in seeing the changes that had taken place, since they were accustomed to changes. As they recognized the promise of new experiences, their eyes sparkled brightly and they asked, "What are we going to do?"

DISCUSSION

I invited them to sit down on the floor and discuss it with me. We talked a little about spring, and how it makes you feel inside when you see all the growing things getting ready to say, "Hello, I'm here."

Some of the children's comments were "It makes me feel I like you," "I want to sing happy," and "I think I want to scream!"

I replied, "I'll tell you what I would like you to do. You can use any of the things you see around the room. Listen to the music, make up an art dance, and while you're dancing, I'll look into your faces and then I'll know how you feel. You may use the paints, the crayons, the chalks, the glue, or the musical instruments. You may use any of the pieces of paper, but you must share everything and take turns. Paint, or color, or glue, or dance, or sing. You may do all of these things whenever you feel like doing them and you may do them any way you like to do them."

CHOICES AND LIMITS

The children were quickly on their feet, ready to make their own discoveries. To explore. To experience. To respond.

The children were not told, "Do whatever you want to do." This only leads to confusion and uncertainty. The success of this experiment was at least partially due to the clearly defined limits that had been set. The children were given a choice of materials to use within the framework of a carefully structured environment. But they were told only that they could paint, color, glue, sing, or dance. They were given instructions, but they were still free to do those things when they felt like doing them and in the way they wanted to do them. On their own initiative the children one by one took off their shoes and began to dance around the room.

It was truly a joyful expression of creative freedom.

The only assistance the children required was starting the nonautomatic record player over and over again. Near the end of the activity, an adult directed the cleanup, which was also done to the same music as part of the whole experience.

THE EXPERIENCE

For 45 minutes, the children expressed their moods, released their tensions, and worked out their feelings through art and music. Everywhere movement and rhythm were accompanied by experimentation and involvement. The various types of activities constantly interacted. The children responded particularly deeply because they had all participated for at least several months in creative developmental art activities. The children had been constantly challenged to make maximum use of their bodies and their minds as integrated wholes. When the Art Dance was suggested, the children were able to accept the opportunity naturally and to participate with the full enjoyment of those who had been helped to see beyond the surface of the environment.

Results
In addition to the learning that usually occurs during various creative art activities, the Art Dance helps children to
  1. increase their auditory-motor and visual perception and
  2. experience a general overall growth in sensory awareness as body, mind, music, and media all flow together.

DISCOVERY CORNER
The Discovery Corner is a special area of the classroom that contains materials that children do not ordinarily use or that they are allowed to use only occasionally. The area can be just large enough for only one child at a time, or it can be an entire table set up so that several children can work at once.

Individual sets of materials can be prepared for the children or taken from a supply center to an area where they may want to work. Or the children may select the items desired and make up an individual set. It can be set up by the teacher, or it can be part of the day-to-day free-play activities.

Materials

The materials can be put in trays, lazy susans, divided boxes, or similar containers. Just be sure that the materials are offered in a neat, colorful, and attractive way. Include such items as

ballpoint pens	oil pastels	plastic triangle
carbon paper	paper clips	ruler
cellophane	paper fasteners	scissors
charcoal	paper punch	stapler
colored pencils	paper	string
glue	paste	watercolor pan and
Kleenex	pinking shears	brushes
metallic paper	pipe cleaners	yarn or thread

Add any other materials you wish. The greater use of your imagination in equipping and setting up the Discovery Corner, the greater the children's use of their imaginations in discovering for themselves what to do with the materials provided.

Results

In addition to the learning that usually occurs during various creative art activities, the Discovery Corner helps children to
1. *make choices,*
2. *develop eye-hand coordination, and*
3. *practice imaginative thinking.*

IMAGINATION BOX

The Imagination Box is an attractively decorated box or other container that you have prepared for use by one or two children at a time. It is similar to the Discovery Corner in that it is a means of enlarging the children's experiences in self-discovery and experimentation. You may have several such boxes, each one individually prepared. In the box you place selected collections of surprises with which the children can create their own happening. The children are not told to "make something" with the materials, but they usually will. However, they may prefer simply to investigate, arrange, and play with the items. This, too, is an enriching experience.

Materials

Feathers

Styrofoam squares

Pipe cleaners

Strips of construction paper

Two pieces of felt

Some ribbon

Several pieces of metallic
     paper from a wallpaper
     book

Small box of sequins

A jar of glitter

Felt scraps

A paper punch

White glue

Yarn

Graph paper

An almost empty bottle of
     red india ink with a good
     watercolor brush

Gummed paper scraps

Pieces of cardboard

Masking tape

Cellophane tape

Scissors

Your collection can be fantastic. Let your ideas run free. Just be sure that whatever you put in the box will stick or color or mark or fasten. For example, if the box contained only wax paper and watercolors, the children couldn't invent anything. They would only discover that watercolor won't adhere to wax paper.

If the materials are presented with care and in an attractive manner, the children will handle them with care. Children learn by example. To develop in children the ability to direct their own behavior, remember that they will pattern that behavior after the behavior and attitudes of others in their environment, both at school and away from school. Their creative attitudes are directly dependent on your creative attitude.

Results

In addition to the learning that usually occurs during various creative art activities, the Discovery Corner, like the Imagination Box, helps children to

1. *make choices,*
2. *develop eye-hand coordination,*
3. *practice imaginative thinking,*
4. *build self-esteem, since they realize they have the freedom to use their own ideas,*
5. *reinforce all the other things they have learned through ongoing creative art projects, and*
6. *encourage the development of the ability to innovate with available materials.*

Integrating Creative Art into the Curriculum

The new cash register had arrived, and Mrs. Blue was excitedly showing it to her prekindergarten class of 4-year-olds. She asked who knew where cash registers were used. "To buy things!" "At the store!" "At my dad's garage!" "Where you get shoes!" "At the market!" "When you buy ice cream!" "Where Mom gets milk!" "At the beer place!" "When we go to a restaurant!" "At McDonalds!" The children shouted out these and other locations almost simultaneously. There was some conversation about why cash registers are used, and then the cash register was passed around so that everyone could have a turn opening the cash drawer and making the bell ring. Mrs. Blue asked, "How can we use this in our room?" Again, there were many ideas. Several of the children felt it should be for a supermarket. One by one, most of the others agreed, and the teacher said, "Well, since you want to make a supermarket, I think we should go visit one. Tomorrow we'll take a walk to the market on 40th Street and get ideas for how to plan our own market. Meanwhile, we'll keep the cash register on this shelf over here, and you may take turns one at a time practicing how to use it, so that you'll be able to do a good job when you work at the market."

A TWO-MONTH ART HAPPENING

Through the medium of creative art experiences, it is possible to slowly build various areas of the curriculum into one many-faceted unit with multiple learning opportunities. Such units are appropriate for young children because they are not confined to a single topic in which some children may not have interest, but rather they offer many opportunities for taking off into individual tangents and interests.

THE SUPERMARKET

Several areas of study had been going on in our school over a period of weeks. The introduction into the classroom of the new cash register and its placement in the block cupboard, plus a walk to a supermarket, led to an ever-growing, ever-changing play market mushrooming from the block-building corner out into the center of the classroom. Each day a new construction expanded the structure into an ever-more elaborate complex of many rooms and divisions.

In the hallway, just outside the classroom but still within range of the teacher's supervision, a few children at a time were allowed to play with some large refrigerator packing cartons that had been given to the school. The boxes were large enough for a child to walk into. They were used as tunnels, hideouts, trains, wigwams, spaceships, and many other intriguing, magical things.

(**Note:** It may be illegal in your state or city to have empty refrigerator-sized or other large combustible cartons in the classroom. This project may have to be done in an outdoor area. Check with your local fire department. Also, investigate the possibility of applying a fireproofing finish to the boxes.)

Leo, Kira, and John making a building-block construction.

THE TELEPHONE BOOTH

During these same weeks, the teachers had been helping all the children to learn their home telephone numbers. This led to a study of the telephone, practice in how to answer it, and much play with both toy and real phones. One day the teacher made a bulletin board display of telephone booths. As a result, the children decided they would like to make a "real" telephone booth. One child suggested using one of the packing cartons and painting it. The other children agreed.

The floor was covered with newspaper, and a box was brought in to be painted. The teacher provided red liquid tempera, red powdered tempera, two cans of condensed milk, 2-, 3-, and 4-inch brushes, and several containers to mix the paint in. (Using canned milk to thin out paint gives it a hard, slightly glossy finish that, when dry, does not rub off.) The children took turns working on the telephone booth, and each one mixed his or her own supply of paint.

Results
By painting this large box, the children
1. *became more aware of such concepts as top, bottom, and the other side,*
2. *discovered that it takes longer to paint a big cardboard box than a small one,*
3. *learned that the larger the brush, the less time it takes to cover an area,*
4. *found that it took two coats of paint to cover the printing on the box,*
5. *realized the box looked better if the paint was applied with long, smooth strokes rather than with short dabs, and*
6. *discovered that splashed paint needs to be wiped up right away before it dries because the addition of milk forms a hard-finish paint that can not be easily cleaned off.*

Jill and Stevie painting the telephone booth.

After the box was painted, the teacher cut a door into one side of the box and then a window into the door. She fastened a plastic toy wall telephone to one wall of the box with 3" bolts (heads on the outside). All the children wrote their names and phone numbers in a telephone book that hung in the booth. The children placed a hollow block inside the box for a seat.

THE REDESIGNED SUPERMARKET

The chief engineers of the supermarket project decided that the phone booth should be located in their "shopping center." When they saw that the phone booth towered far above their wooden blocks, the children decided they needed a new kind of supermarket. The blocks were stacked away and replaced with the remaining cartons.

The teacher first cut one side out of each of the boxes to make doorways. Then the children selected a bright lavender paint to use on the boxes. (Condensed milk was added to the paint as before.) All the children took a turn painting the boxes with the creamy milk-and-paint mixture. The lavender paint on the light brown corrugated cardboard produced a fluorescent effect that the children found exhilarating. Most adults thought that the lavender clashed somewhat with the red of the telephone booth, but the children thought the color combination was quite beautiful.

Results
This activity reinforced what the children had learned when they painted the telephone booth, and it taught them some new things. They
> 1. *discovered that the corners of a very big box were just as small as the corners of a little box and just as hard to get paint into,*
> 2. *found that it takes much longer to paint both the inside and*

the outside of a box than it does to paint only the outside,
and

3. *realized that the lavender paint didn't dry to as glossy a
finish as the red paint had because of the white paint that
had been added to it.*

STOCKING THE SUPERMARKET

Notes were sent home to the children's families asking them to
save their empty food containers for the class to use in stocking
the supermarket. There was a great response, and the children
spent many hours sorting, stacking, arranging, rearranging,
categorizing, and pricing the packages. (The packages were
priced 1, 2, or 3.) The containers were arranged on shelves that
had been improvised from hollow blocks placed along the walls
of each of the refrigerator boxes.

Since everything had to be stored away each Friday, the
classifying and arranging began anew each Monday. Therefore, all the children had many opportunities to participate in
all aspects of the entire experience. They learned that the
pictures on the labels of the packages could help them decide
where an item belonged. Cheese, eggs, and milk belong in the
dairy department. Ice cream could be kept in either the dairy
department or with the frozen foods. Soap powder should not
be stored next to the dry cereal, even though the boxes contain-
ing the two products are similar in size, shape, and color.

Results
*Through the arrangement and rearrangement of the supermar-
ket, the children*

1. *internalized their understanding of important concepts
such as sorting, classifying, and comparing according to
size, shape, and color and*

2. *became aware of the lettering on the labels and the idea of separating various types of food items.*

To create a new activity around the supermarket theme, the teacher drew horizontal lines on some posterboard to represent shelves. She asked the children to look through magazines and cut out pictures of food to paste on the make-believe shelves. However, the children were absolutely not interested in this kind of categorizing. It was a rather dull activity in comparison to the joy they had experienced in being "hands-on" creators. The project was abandoned.

FRUITS AND VEGETABLES

The children, however, were intensely interested in the next activity, which was making their own fruits and vegetables.

Materials
Heavy paper such as tagboard, or even heavier (a good-quality 80-lb. drawing paper would work well)
Fingerpaint in rich mixtures of red, green, yellow, orange, and deep purple
Black crayons
Scissors
Glue
Several posterboards with rows of slots cut into them

Procedure
The children painted each sheet of the heavy paper one color. Each child did several pieces, using colors of his or her choice.

When the papers were dry, they used the black crayons to outline their versions of fruit and vegetable shapes on the papers, which they then cut out.

After the shapes were cut out, we had a fascinating assortment of imaginative, odd-shaped, but fresh-looking produce. The various items were neatly arranged in the slots that had been cut into the posterboards.

THE ACTIVITY

For several weeks, each morning's activities centered around the store. The cash register was expertly operated by one child after another. This was an extremely popular activity, so cashiers were changed frequently during shopping hours. The shoppers spent a great deal of time getting dressed for their excursions. Gloves, hats, purses, and other items all came from the dress-up supply.

The children experimented with many different types of items to use for pretend money. Sometimes, real pennies were provided.

Eventually, the food boxes had been sorted, stacked, bought, and sold so many times that they needed mending and patching. Some had been handled, inspected, opened, and closed so often that they were beginning to lose their shape.

THE CLOSE-OUT SALE

We decided it was time to have a close-out sale. The boxes were transferred to the art supply table. Each child was allowed to select three favorite boxes to paint. Dark brown or dark blue paint with a little white added seemed to cover the printing on the packages better than the other colors. Light colors of paint did not work well at all. Some of the packages had waxy or foil coatings, so the teacher added a little detergent to the paint to make it adhere better. (She could have also used wheat paste.) The small size of most of the packages challenged the children's

James, Terri, Anne, Roger, Michael, and Stephen painting food containers.

muscular control as they tried to apply the paint neatly with a relatively large brush. The children faced the demanding problem of figuring out how to paint all sides of the boxes without smearing the sides already painted. But when they succeeded, they were delighted to discover that their old, worn boxes looked fresh and new.

BOX SCULPTURING

A few days later the children arrived to find the classroom set up for a new activity: Box Sculpturing. On one table, the freshly painted supermarket containers were lined up in a row according to size. On another table, several bottles of white glue and rubber cement, cellophane tape, masking tape, scissors, string, and yarn were placed on a large aluminum foil baking pan.

The children were told they could choose any of the containers and fasten them together however they wished. Many of the projects took several days. No one seemed to have any trouble mastering the mechanics involved. If they were unable to glue one piece to another, they taped it. If taping didn't work, they would try to hold it with their fingers while the glue set. Each new variation on this box sculpture introduced a new problem to solve.

Results

In doing box sculptures, the children gained valuable experience in

1. *determining spatial and size relationships,*
2. *discovering how physical objects fit together,*
3. *experimenting with the principles of mechanics,*
4. *substituting one material for another to achieve a desired goal, and*
5. *exploring concepts of balance, gravity, and design.*

THE CITY

As a final project before school closed for the summer, the older children decided to construct a city. The teacher supplied some new cardboard boxes of many sizes and shapes along with a tempera-detergent paint mixture, white glue, masking tape, and other fastening materials. The teacher recognized every child's growing desire to produce representational objects and knew that with their experience in box sculpture and painting, she could let them proceed freely with their own plans. The result was a delightful collection of houses, buildings, and cars.

THE MURAL

To complete the project, the children painted a large background mural to hang behind their city. At first glance the mural seemed to be totally abstract, but a careful examination

The Cardboard City.

revealed an imaginative painting of trees, flowers, sky, and ground totally created by children who were culminating a year of activities similar to those found throughout this book.

Creative Developmental Art

The box building, from the first beginning play with floor blocks through to the building of a cardboard city, were all part of the creative developmental art experience. It was creative because the ideas originated with the children. Each experience served to motivate a succeeding experience. Once the flow of creative thought was started, imaginations became active and inventive actions took place. The activities were developmental because they changed in response to the developing needs and abilities of the children.

Throughout, the teacher served as a facilitator, rather than a critic, thus adding to the children's ability to be artistically productive.

Results

Building with boxes gives the children opportunities to

1. *carry, haul, stack, pack, unpack, classify, and categorize,*
2. *participate in group planning and thus increase ease and self-confidence in social relationships,*
3. *progress from using materials symbolically to creating representational and recognizable shapes, forms, and objects,*
4. *expand their ability to use their own imaginative ideas because the teacher maintained an environment in which the children were allowed maximum creative freedom,*
5. *increase their self-esteem as they applied skills and ideas that they had acquired through home and school experiences.*

APPENDIX A

MATERIALS FOR COLLAGE AND CONSTRUCTION

Listed below are some suggestions to help you build a collection of materials for collages, constructions, and other art projects. From this list you may want to select items to help teach certain concepts. Of course, you do not have to keep all of these items on hand. These suggestions, however, should help you accumulate an interesting and varied collection.

Acetate, colored
Acorns
Acorn tops
Allspice
Almonds
Aluminum foil
Apple seeds
Artificial flowers

Ball bearings
Balsa wood
Bamboo
Bark
Beads
Beans
Berry baskets
Bias tape
Blotter paper
Bolts and nuts
Bones
Bottle caps
Bottles
Boxes, small

Brads
Braiding
Broken parts
Broken toys
Broom straws
Buckles
Burlap scraps

Cancelled stamps
Candles
Candy wrappers
Cardboard scraps
Cardboard tubes
Carpet samples
Carpet warp
Cellophane scraps
Cellophane tape
Chains
Chalk
Checkers
Cigar bands
Clock parts
Clothespins

Cloves
Coffee filters
Coins
Combs, broken
Construction paper
  scraps
Con-Tact paper
Cord
Corks
Corn husks
Corn kernels
Corrugated card-
  board scraps
Costume jewelry
Cotton batting
Cotton puffs
Crepe paper scraps
Crystals

Dice
Dominoes
Drinking straws
Drapery samples

Dried beans and peas
Dried flowers and grasses
Dried seeds
Driftwood
Dry cereals

Easter grass
Egg cartons
Eggshells
Embroidery thread
Emery boards
Envelopes
Evergreen branches
Eyelets
Excelsior

Fabrics
Faucet washers
Feathers
Felt scraps
Filters
Fishing lures
Fish tank gravel (hooks removed)
Flash bulbs, used
Flint paper
Flocking
Florist's tape, foil, and foam
Flowers, artificial
Flowers, dried

Foam packing of many shapes
Fur samples

Gauze
Gift wrap paper
Gimp nails
Glass beads
Glass mosaic rocks and pieces
Glitter
Gold jewelry parts
Gold thread
Grains
Gravels
Greeting cards
Grocery bags
Gummed labels
Gummed notebook paper reinforcers
Gummed paper

Hairnets
Hairpins
Hair rollers
Hardware scraps
Hat trimmings
Holiday trimmings
Hooks

Ice cream sticks
Inner tube scraps

Jar tops

Jewelry pieces
Jewelry wire
Junk of all kinds
Jute

Key rings
Keys
Key tabs

Lace
Laminated items
Leather scraps
Leaves
Lentils
Lids
Linoleum scraps

Mailing tubes
Map pins
Marbles
Masonite
Meat trays, paper
Meat trays, styrofoam
Meat trays, transparent plastic
Mesh netting
Metal scraps
Metal shavings
Mirrors
Mosaic rocks
Mosaic tiles
Mosquito netting
Moss, dried

Muffin liners
Muslin scraps

Nails
Newspapers
Noodles, cooked
Noodles, dry
Nut cups
Nuts
Nylon scraps

Oilcloth scraps
Orange seeds
Orange sticks
Origami paper
Ornaments

Packing styrofoam
Paint chips
Paper baking cups
Paper clips
Paper dots from
    computer paper
Paper fastener
    reinforcements
Paper products of
    all kinds
Paper tubes
Pebbles
Pill bottles
Pillboxes
Pinecones
Pine needles
Ping-pong balls

Pins of all kinds
Pipe cleaners
Plastic bottles
Plastic foam
Plastic pieces from
    old toys
Popcorn
Popsicle sticks
Potatoes
Pumpkin seeds

Q-tips
Quartz crystals
Quills

Raffia
Recording tape
Rhinestones
Ribbons
Rice
Rickrack
Rocks
Rock salt
Rope pieces
Rubber bands
Rubber tubing

Safety pins
Salt crystals
Sandpaper
Sawdust
Scouring pads
Screening, plastic
    or wire

Screws
Seals, gummed
Seam binding
Seashells
Seed pods
Seeds
Sequins
Shoelaces
Sponge scraps
Stamps, magazine
    contest
Stickers, gummed

Tape, cellophane
Tape, cloth
Tape, masking
Tape, plastic
Tape, sewing
Telephone wire
Thistles
Threads
Tiles
Tinkertoy parts
Tissue paper scraps
Tongue depressors
Toothbrushes
Toothpicks
Torn paper scraps
Twigs
Twine
Typewriter ribbon
    spools

Velveteen

Velvet scraps
Vermiculite

Wallpaper
Washers
Wax candles
Weeds
Wooden beads
Wooden dowels
Wooden wheels

Wood scraps
Wood shavings
Wool

Yarns

Zippers

APPENDIX B

SCROUNGING FOR ART MATERIALS

Many free or inexpensive materials for your creative art program are obtainable through scrounging. The following are suggestions of resources where you might look for various materials.

Architects
Discarded paper (do not use blueprint paper, because some people are allergic to the dye)

Art Materials Suppliers
Broken packages
Close-out materials
Discarded materials

Beaches
Shells
Rocks

Cabinet Makers
Wood scraps
Wood turnings, knobs, and other parts for cabinet and furniture finishing
Sawdust

Camera and Photography Businesses
Empty film cans
Used flashbulbs

Carpeting Suppliers
Carpet samples

Linoleum scraps
Discarded carpet tape

Clock and Watch Repair Shops

Discarded clocks and watches
Parts from old clocks and watches
Discarded leather bands

Dairies

Empty milk, cream, cottage cheese, ice cream, and egg
cartons

Department Stores

Display materials
Discarded trimmings
Discarded stationery
Discarded boxes

Drugstores and Pharmacies

Discarded display materials (posters, trims, etc.)
Empty plastic and cardboard containers
Broken packages of nontoxic materials such as cotton,
cotton swabs, tongue depressors, and combs

Electronic Equipment Repair or Supply Shops

Packing blocks
Styrofoam packing pieces
Used rubber stamps and ink pads (ask all businesses for
these)
Computer cards and paper
Wire and cords

Flower Shops

Discarded trimming materials
Discarded cellophane, colored aluminum foil, and other
paper
Dried plants and flowers

Frame Shops
Miscut mat board
Centers from mat board frames

Furniture Stores
Catalogs
Samples of upholstery fabrics

Garden Shops
Broken tile pieces
Trimmings

Glass and Window Repair Businesses
Chips of broken glass, especially colored (handle with care)
Discarded materials

Hardware and Home Repair Suppliers
Nuts, bolts, nails, screws
Other discarded small items
Mismatched paint (for painting containers for supplies)

Homes
Groceries, such as nuts, cereals, spices, seeds, and pastas
   (you may also be able to get contributions of bulk products
   from grocery stores)
Packaging materials
Findings from the "junk drawer," such as broken pieces,
   wires, hardware, scraps

Ice Cream Dealers
Ice cream cartons, all sizes, especially 5-gallon size

Lamps and Lighting Dealers
Wooden dowels that support lamp shades in packing
Other packing materials

Libraries
Old date cards
Date stamps and other stamps
Ink pads

Lumber Companies
Molding and trim materials
Wood scraps
Sawdust
Scraps of other building materials

Medical Offices, Hospitals, Dentists
Discarded cardboard and plastic containers
Tubing
Plaster of paris

Mountains and Countryside
Pinecones
Leaves
Twigs
Acorns and other seeds
Seed pods
Reeds
Weeds
Gravel

Newspaper Companies
Ends of rolls of newsprint

Paint Suppliers
Color folders
Paint chips
Wallpaper books

Printing Companies
Ends of rolls of paper

Cut ends of printing paper and cardboard
Discarded paper
Misprinted paper

Shoe Stores
Shoe boxes

Tile Setters
Broken and discarded tiles

Yarn and Yardage Shops
Broken packages of yarns
Samples of yarns and fabrics
Color samples
Findings, such as rickrack, buttons, threads, and spools
Remnants
Catalogs and pattern books
Cardboard tubes that some yardage is wrapped around

If a potential supplier promises to save materials for you, leave a convenient container for them, should they want one. When someone has agreed to save materials for you, it is your responsibility to go to them (don't telephone) to see if they have done so.

Parents are often very cooperative in helping you to obtain materials—especially if they can do so from their place of employment. A parent who doesn't work but needs to find a way to earn some tuition credit could assist you in scrounging for materials.

When anything, however small, has been contributed, be sure to write a letter of thanks. Let suppliers know of your sincere appreciation and that you are telling people to patronize them.

INDEX

Entries printed in *italic* type refer to illustrations. Entries printed in SMALL CAPITAL LETTERS refer to activities and projects. References to the learning and development that result from the creative art program are cross-referenced under "Conceptual understandings" and "Results (skills and awareness)."